Eugene J. Hall   English For Careers

The Language of Electrical and Electronic Engineering in English

Regents Publishing Company, Inc.

Illustrations by Bernie Case

Copyright © 1977 by
Regents Publishing Company, Inc.

Published by
Regents Publishing Company, Inc.
2 Park Avenue
New York, N.Y. 10016

Printed in the United States of America

ISBN 0-88345-301-0

TABLE OF CONTENTS

FOREWORD   v

UNIT ONE
The Engineering Profession   1

UNIT TWO
Electrons and Electricity   14

UNIT THREE
Electric Currents and Circuits   26

UNIT FOUR
Electromagnetism   40

UNIT FIVE
Electricity and Electronics   54

UNIT SIX
Radio Waves and Vacuum Tubes   64

UNIT SEVEN
Miniaturization and Microminiaturization   77

UNIT EIGHT
Electrical and Electronic Engineering in the Future   89

INDEX OF SPECIAL TERMS   97

OTHER TITLES IN THE ENGLISH FOR CAREERS SERIES

The Language of Air Travel in English: Ground Services	# 18500
The Language of Air Travel in English: In-Flight Services	# 18501
The Language of the Petroleum Industry in English	# 18502
The Language of Computer Programming in English	# 18503
The Language of International Finance in English: Money and Banking	# 18504
The Language of the Air Force in English	# 18505
The Language of the Army in English	# 18506
The Language of the Navy in English	# 18507
The Language of Tourism in English	# 18508
The Language of Hotels in English	# 18509
The Language of Restaurants and Catering in English	# 18510
The Language of Hospital Services in English	# 18511
The Language of Accounting in English	# 18512
The Language of National Defense in English	# 18513
The Language of Atomic Energy in English	# 18514
The Language of Chemical Engineering in English	# 18515
The Language of Civil Engineering in English	# 18516
The Language of Mechanical Engineering in English	# 18518
The Language of the Merchant Marine in English	# 18519
The Language of Advertising and Merchandising in English	# 18520
The Language of Mining and Metallurgy in English	# 18521
The Language of International Trade in English: Importing and Exporting	# 18522
The Language of Aviation in English: Flying and Traffic Control	# 18523
The Language of Agriculture in English	# 18524

FOREWORD

This book is one of a series of texts called *English for Careers*. The series is intended to introduce students of English as a foreign language to the particular language of different professional and vocational fields. The career areas covered are those in which English is widely used throughout the world—computer programming, air travel, international finance, the petroleum industry, and in this book, electrical and electronic engineering.

Each book in the series serves to give the student an introduction in English to the vocational area in which he or she is interested. *The Language of Electrical and Electronic Engineering* gives some of the theoretical background on which practical applications of electrical energy are based. There is also a discussion of the developments that are expected to take place in this field in the coming years.

The books in the series are intended for students at the high intermediate or advanced level, who are acquainted with a majority of the structural patterns of English. Thus, from the point of view of English as a foreign language, each book is designed to aid students in mastering the vocabulary of an area of specialization, and to give them practice using the vocabulary in conversational situations. The goal is for students to improve their ability to communicate in English, particularly with others in their field.

Each unit of this book begins with a glossary of special terms in which words and expressions used in electrical and electronic engineering are defined. The special terms are followed by a vocabulary practice section, which tests the student's comprehension of the terms and gives practice in their use. In the reading passage, these terms are used again within a contextual frame of reference. The reading passage is followed by questions for discussion, which give the student the opportunity to use in a communicative situation both the vocabulary items and the structural patterns that have occurred in the reading.

Each unit ends with a review section of one or two exercises. Some exercises test the student's ability to recall the special vocabulary. Other exercises pose problems the student might encounter in the field—he or she might be asked to identify some of the symbols used in diagrams of electric circuits, or to discuss the advantages or disadvantages of using certain kinds of equipment. In doing these exercises, the student will again be practicing the specialized vocabulary and the structural patterns used with them.

A great deal of successful language learning comes from experiences in which the learning is largely unconscious. In offering these books, we hope that the students' interest in the career information presented will facilitate their learning to communicate more easily in English.

EUGENE J. HALL
Washington, D.C.

UNIT ONE
THE ENGINEERING PROFESSION

Special Terms

Engineering: The practical application of the findings of theoretical science. An *engineer* is a member of the engineering profession. The term "engineer" is also used to refer to a person who operates or maintains certain kinds of equipment—a railroad locomotive engineer, for example. In that case, the person referred to is a technician rather than a professional engineer.

Profession: An occupation such as law, medicine, or engineering which requires specialized education of four or more years at the university level.

Civil engineers.

Civil Engineering: The branch of engineering that deals with planning structures for civilian use such as roads, buildings, bridges, and water supply and sewage systems. *Military engineering* is concerned with similar projects for military use.

Mining and Metallurgy: The branch of engineering that deals with extracting metal ores from the earth and refining them.

A mining engineer.

A mechanical engineer.

A chemical engineer.

Mechanical Engineering: The branch of engineering that deals with machines and their uses.

Chemical Engineering: The branch of engineering that deals with the processes involved in reactions among the elements, the basic natural substances. *Petroleum engineering* deals specifically with processes involving petroleum.

Electrical and Electronic Engineering: The branch of engineering that deals with the processes and devices derived from the movement of electrons.

Nuclear Engineering: A modern branch of engineering that deals with finding practical uses for the processes that result from breaking up the nuclei of atoms.

Atom: The basic particle of matter of which the chemical elements are made up. An atom consists of a *nucleus* around which smaller particles called *electrons* orbit. Electrons and the particles in the nucleus are called *subatomic particles*. The plural of nucleus is *nuclei*.

Electron Microscope: A microscope is a device which magnifies small objects so that they are visible. An electron microscope uses a beam of

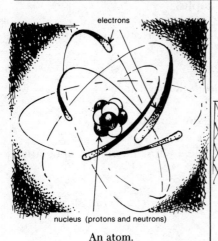

An atom.

Electrical engineers.

electrons instead of light to magnify images.

Particle Accelerator: A device that speeds up subatomic particles. It is used for research in atomic physics.

Empirical Information: Information based on observation and experience rather than on theoretical knowledge.

Nuclear engineers.

Aqueduct: A structure that is used to carry water over long distances.

Quantification: Putting data (pieces of information) into exact mathematical terms.

Vocabulary Practice

1. What does *engineering* mean?

2. How does a railroad locomotive engineer differ from a professional engineer?

3. What is a *profession?* Give examples.

4. What does *civil engineering* deal with? How does it differ from *military engineering?*

5. What does *mining and metallurgy* deal with?

6. What is *mechanical engineering* concerned with?

7. What does *chemical engineering* deal with? Name one specialized branch of chemical engineering.

8. What is the special area of *electrical and electronic engineering?*

9. What is *nuclear engineering?*

10. What is an *atom?* What are its different parts? What is a *sub-atomic particle?*

11. What is a *microscope?* How does an *electron microscope* differ from an ordinary microscope?

12. What is a *particle accelerator?* In what kind of research is it used?

13. What is *empirical information?*

14. What is an *aqueduct* used for?

15. What is meant by *quantification?*

The Engineering Profession

Engineering is as old as history. One of the earliest engineers was Imhotep, who designed the stepped pyramid of Sakkhara in Egypt in the twenty-seventh century B.C. Mankind could not have emerged from a primitive hunting and gathering existence without the engineering skills needed to create tools, metal refining processes, buildings, roads, and irrigation and sanitation systems. As human society has grown more complex, the need for many different engineering skills

The construction of a pyramid in ancient Egypt.

Engineering has a great influence on our daily lives.

has multiplied. In our era, engineering has significantly changed our daily existence. Machines and communication and transportation systems not only do a great deal of our work but have also increased our capacity for work. Indeed, the social changes that have been created by engineers are so great that our society has not yet completely come to grips with all that they mean.

Engineers make practical application of the findings of theoretical, or "pure," sciences such as physics or chemistry. A three-part distinction is sometimes made between theoretical science, applied science, and engineering. The research of theoretical science is done primarily to add to our knowledge of nature. Little consideration is given to the possible applications of research findings. Applied science is concerned with discovering ways to use the knowledge of theoretical science. Engineering carries the research one step further by devising workable processes based on the discoveries of applied science.

An example of this three-part system is in the development of nuclear energy. Chemists and physicists studied the structure of the *atom* over a long period of time. They learned that atoms of uranium-235 could be split into two nearly equal parts, releasing a great deal of energy in the process. Then, under the pressures of World War II, applied science took over the research to find a military use for this release of energy. Applied scientists discovered that it was possible to create a chain reaction, a controlled release of energy that continued by itself. Then, engineers together with scientists began to work out the difficult and complex systems that made the atomic bomb a reality. After the war, scientists and engineers again worked as a team to find ways of putting atomic energy to work for peaceful purposes such as generating electric power.

This is a comparatively clear-cut example of the distinction between what might be called the "three sciences." However, as our knowledge of science has grown, engineers have begun to play a greater role in all phases of scientific work. Devices such as *electron microscopes* and *particle accelerators*, designed and built by engineers, are used in the search for basic information. At the same time, more and more engineers are members of scientific teams involved not only in the development of workable machines and systems, but in all aspects of research.

For thousands of years, engineers based their work on *empirical information*—information that depended on observation and experience rather than on theoretical knowledge. Many ancient structures, such as the *aqueducts* of Rome, have survived because they were built with greater strength than would be considered necessary by modern standards, which are based on scientific research and complex mathematical calculations.

The earliest engineering work was in the fields that we would now call civil and military engineering, and mining and metallurgy. *Civil engineering* is concerned with the construction of buildings, roads, bridges, and irrigation and sanitation systems for civil as opposed to military use. *Mining and metallurgy* involves finding deposits of metal-bearing ores and developing systems for refining them. So important is this branch of engineering that mankind's progress in civilization is marked by the names of the metals in use at different periods of history—the Bronze Age and the Iron Age.

The modern age, which began in the sixteenth and seventeenth centuries, has brought an explosion of science in every field—physics, chemistry, astronomy, and physiology—and has introduced new fields, such as nuclear physics. One of the reasons for this rapid increase in scientific knowledge has been the use of the experimental method to verify theories. At least as important has been the use of *quantification*—putting the data acquired through experimentation into exact mathematical terms. Mathematics is the language of modern engineering.

As scientific knowledge increased, so did its practical applications. The eighteenth century witnessed the beginning of the Industrial Revolution, when machines began to take over more of the work that had previously been done manually. In the nineteenth century scientific research and the practical application of its results progressed rapidly. This brought a greater understanding of natural forces as well as substantial changes in the way people lived.

Another result of the growth of knowledge was an increase in the number of scientific and engineering specialties. By the end of the nineteenth century, civil engineering, *mechanical engineering*, and mining and metallurgy had been established, and courses were being offered in the newer specialties of *electrical* and *chemical engineering*. The number of specialties has continued to grow right up to the present, with the establishment of such disciplines as aerospace, *nuclear*, *petroleum*, industrial, and *electronic engineering*. Some of these have developed from older disciplines—petroleum from chemical engineering, and electronic from electrical engineering.

Because of the variety and number of engineering fields today, there are often many different kinds of engineers working on large projects such as space exploration and nuclear power development. On such projects, the engineer is usually a member of a team headed by a systems engineer, a person who coordinates the contributions made by all the different disciplines. Because teamwork enters into so many engineering projects, being able to work easily with others is an important qualification for engineers.

A final result of the increase in scientific knowledge is that engineering has become a *profession*. A profession is an occupation like law or medicine that requires specialized advanced education; they are often called the "learned professions." Until the nineteenth century, engineers were for the most part craftsmen who learned their skills through apprenticeship, or on-the-job training. Today, becoming an engineer requires at least a four- or five-year university course leading to a Bachelor of Science or an engineering degree. More and more engineers, especially those engaged in research, go on to get a master's or doctor's degree. Even those engineers who do not study for advanced degrees must keep up with changes in their own field and related areas. All of this means that an engineer's education is never really finished; he or she must be willing to be involved in a constant learning process.

The word "engineer" has two uses in English. One, as we have indicated, refers to the professional engineer who has a university degree and an education in mathematics, science, and one of the engineering specialties. "Engineer," however, is also used to describe a person who operates or maintains an engine or a machine. A good example of this is the railroad locomotive engineer who runs our trains. These engineers are essentially technicians rather than professional engineers, the kind we will refer to in this book.

There are two other important considerations for today's engineers. First, they work with management and government officials who are very cost-conscious and demand that engineering systems be workable not only from a technical, but also from an economic point of view. Therefore, an engineer must be able to develop his or her ideas within the financial realities of a particular project.

Second, the general public has become much more aware in recent years of the social and environmental consequences of engineering projects. For much of the nineteenth and twentieth centuries, engineering was the most visible part of science, and since the general attitude was that all science was good, engineering progress was usually accepted without reservation. Today, people are showing greater concern about possible dangers resulting from advances in engineering. Generating electric power by means of nuclear energy has not progressed as rapidly as many scientists and engineers predicted, partially because of the public's new awareness of the human and environmental dangers involved. Engineers cannot work in a scientific vacuum but must also take into account the social consequences of their work. We have, after all, described engineering as a profession which makes practical application of the findings of theoretical science. A successful engineer must include in a definition of "practical" the idea that the work should be desirable to society and safe for human beings.

Discussion

1. What is one piece of evidence that we have about how old engineering is?

2. What were some of the products of engineering skills that were necessary in order for mankind to emerge from a primitive existence?

3. How has engineering changed our daily existence?

4. What three-part distinction is often made concerning science? What is the function of each of these parts of science?

5. What example is given of this division of scientific effort into three parts? Can you think of any other examples?

6. Why is the distinction between the three aspects of science no longer so clear-cut?

7. What are two devices often used in basic scientific research?

8. On what kind of information did engineers base their work for thousands of years?

9. Why are many structures from ancient times still in existence?

10. What were the earliest fields of engineering? What kinds of things did each field deal with?

11. What has happened to science since the beginning of the modern age?

12. What are two of the reasons for this rapid increase in scientific knowledge?

13. What effect did the increase in scientific knowledge have in the eighteenth century?

14. What happened to science and engineering in the nineteenth century?

15. In what engineering specialties were courses being offered by the end of the nineteenth century?

16. What are some of the specialties that have developed since then?

17. Why are many engineers members of teams nowadays?

18. Who usually heads a team of engineers?

19. What are some of the "learned professions?" Why has engineering become one of them?

20. What kind of training did most engineers have up until the nineteenth century?

21. What is the minimum education required of an engineer?

22. Why must an engineer be willing to be involved in a constant learning process?

23. What meaning of the term "engineer" will be used in this book? What meaning will not be used?

24. Why must engineers take into account financial realities in developing ideas?

25. How has the public's attitude toward scientific advances changed in recent years?

26. What was the public's attitude toward science and engineering throughout much of the nineteenth and twentieth centuries?

27. Why has generating electric power by means of nuclear energy not progressed as rapidly as many scientists and engineers predicted?

28. What else must engineers take into account in their work?

29. What must a successful engineer include in a definition of "practical"?

Review

A. Fill in the spaces in the following sentences with the appropriate word or phrase.

1. _____ can be defined as the practical application of the findings of theoretical science.

2. A railroad locomotive engineer is a _____ rather than a member of a profession.

3. Law, medicine, and engineering are _____ which require specialized education at the university level.

4. In an atom, _____ are in orbit around the _____.

5. The plural of "nucleus" is _____.

6. Planning a water supply system for a big city would probably be the work of _____ engineers.

7. A mining engineer is concerned with finding _____ and extracting them from the earth.

8. _____ engineers are constantly working to improve the internal combustion engines used in automobiles.

9. _____ engineering is the branch of _____ engineering that an engineer working in an oil refinery would probably specialize in.

10. A _____ is used to magnify the image of small objects so that they can be studied.

11. A _____ speeds up subatomic particles for research purposes.

12. The ancient Romans used _____ information based on experience and observation to build their structures.

13. Many of the _____ that carried water in Roman times are still in existence today.

14. Electrical and electronic engineers work with the effects, processes, and devices derived from the _____ of electrons.

15. Quantification means that pieces of information have been put into _____ terms.

B. Below are some of the projects on which an engineer might work. Indicate which branch of engineering (civil, mechanical, chemical, etc.) would be involved. Some of the projects may involve more than one kind of engineering. If so, indicate all of those that you think should be included.

1. Designing a suspension bridge over a large body of water.   _____

2. Finding a new alloy (mixture) of metals that could be used for special purposes.

_____

3. Designing a control system for the safe operation of a nuclear reactor for an electric power station.

_____

4. Designing the wings for a new type of airplane.

_____

5. Designing an automatic switching system for telephone direct-dialing.

_____

6. Installing an automated conveyor belt in a textile factory.

_____

7. Testing the strength of materials to be used for a sports stadium.

_____

8. Designing a rocket for space exploration that will use nuclear-powered electric motors.

_____

9. Designing the process for making plastics from vegetable materials such as soy beans.

_____

10. Designing safety devices in an electric transmission system.

_____

11. Improving the braking system in an automobile.

_____

12. Finding a process for extracting a higher percentage of uranium from uranium ore.

_____

UNIT TWO
ELECTRONS AND ELECTRICITY

Special Terms

Charge: The property of matter which causes it to attract or repel. Electric charges are either *positive* (+) or *negative* (−). Like charges repel each other; unlike charges attract each other.

Static Electricity: Electric charges that accumulate on a material when it is rubbed against another material.

Friction: The resistance offered by two different substances when rubbed together. Static electricity is produced by friction when electric charges are removed from one substance and transferred to the other.

Electron: A subatomic particle with a negative electric charge. *Planetary electrons* are in orbit around the positively charged nucleus of their atom; *free electrons* have been pulled out of their orbit and are no longer bound to the nucleus.

Proton: A subatomic particle in the nucleus of an atom. It has a positive electric charge.

Neutron: A subatomic particle in the nucleus of an atom. It has no net electric charge.

Atomic Number: The number assigned to the atom of each of the chemical elements. It equals the number of electrons or the number of protons in an atom. Silver, for example, has atomic number 47, so it contains 47 electrons and 47 protons.

Conductor: A material which readily permits the flow of free electrons. Copper is a good conductor.

Insulator: A material which permits a very limited flow of free electrons. Glass is a good insulator.

14

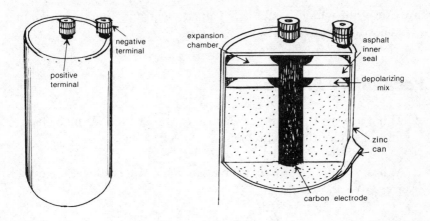

A dry cell.

Energy: The ability to perform work. Energy is required to produce the flow of free electrons.

Current: The flow of free electrons through a conductor.

Cell/Battery: Devices capable of producing a flow of free electrons by means of a chemical reaction. Technically, a battery is made of two or more cells, but the terms are often interchangeable in popular usage.

Circuit: The path followed by an electric current.

Terminal: The point at which a current enters or leaves a circuit.

Electrodes: Plates, usually made of metal, in a cell. They become electrically charged by losing or gaining electrons, thereby enabling the flow of an electric current when the battery is connected to a circuit.

Electrolyte: The chemical solution in which the electrodes in a cell are placed. It is a solution of a salt, an acid, or an alkali.

Cathode: The cell electrode from which electrons enter the electrolyte: the positive terminal of the cell.

Anode: The cell electrode which receives electrons from the electrolyte: the negative terminal of the cell.

Recharging: Renewing the electrical state of cell electrodes by reversing the electric current passing through them. Recharging lengthens the life of the cell.

Electrolytic Process: A process for refining or plating metals which utilizes an electric current passing through an electrolyte. It is also called *electrolysis.*

Ion: An atom which has lost or gained electrons, thereby becoming electrically charged.

Vocabulary Practice

1. What are the two kinds of electric *charges* called? Which charges attract each other and which repel each other?

2. What is *static electricity*? Have you ever observed static electricity? Give an example.

3. What is *friction*? What does it produce?

4. What kind of electric charge does an *electron* have? What are electrons that are in orbit called? What are they called when they are not in orbit?

5. Where are *protons* and *neutrons* found? What is the difference between them?

6. What is the *atomic number* of an element? How many electrons and protons are there in iron, which has atomic number 26?

7. What is the difference between a *conductor* and an *insulator*?

8. What is *energy*? How does it relate to electron flow?

9. What is an electric *current*?

10. What is a *cell* or *battery*? What is the technical difference between them?

11. What is an electric *circuit*?

12. What is a *terminal*?

13. What are *electrodes*? What do they do?

14. What is an *electrolyte*? What does it consist of?

15. What is the difference between a *cathode* and an *anode*?

16. How can a cell be *recharged*?

17. What is the *electrolytic process* used for?

18. What is an *ion*?

Electrons and Electricity

More than two thousand years ago the Greek philosopher Thales observed that when a piece of amber, a hardened gum from trees, was rubbed with a material like wool or fur, it attracted certain other kinds of material. This ability to attract (and also to repel, as it was later discovered) other objects is due to electric *charge*. The phenomenon itself came to be called *static electricity*. "Electricity" comes from the Greek word for amber; "static" indicates that the charge remains stationary, that is, it remains bound to the material that has been charged.

It was many hundreds of years before any further significant observations were made about the phenomenon of static electricity. Then it was discovered that many other materials besides amber could be charged by rubbing, which produced *friction*. A more important discovery was that there were two kinds of electrical charges.

These two kinds of charges were called *positive* and *negative*. A positive charge was indicated by a plus sign (+) and a negative charge by a minus sign (−). These symbols are still in universal use today. It was also discovered that like charges—two positive charges or two negative charges—repelled each other, whereas unlike charges—a positive and a negative charge—attracted each other.

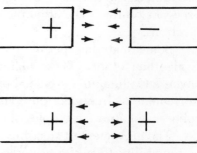

The attraction and repulsion properties of electric charges.

Much later it was learned that the movement of tiny particles of matter called *electrons* caused electricity. The electron is one of the particles that make up atoms, the basic units of matter of which a chemical element is composed. The center of the atom is a nucleus which contains almost the entire weight or mass of the atom. The nucleus itself consists of two different kinds of particles, *protons* and *neutrons*.

Electrons, which have only a very small mass in comparison to protons and neutrons, orbit at a very rapid speed around the nucleus, somewhat in the same manner as the earth and the other planets orbit around the sun. Each atom contains an equal number of electrons and protons but may have a different number of neutrons. Each chemical element has been given an *atomic number* that equals the number of electrons or protons that the atom contains. Hydrogen, the lightest element occurring in nature, has atomic number 1, because an atom of hydrogen contains one electron and one proton. Uranium, one of the heaviest elements, has atomic number 92, for the 92 electrons and 92 protons contained in its atom. Copper, which plays an important part in electricity, has an atom containing 29 electrons and 29 protons, and thus atomic number 29.

The electron, as we have noted, is very light in weight, and can be drawn out of its orbit around the much heavier nucleus. Electrons orbiting farthest from the nucleus are those most easily drawn away. Orbiting electrons are called *planetary electrons*, and those that have been pulled away are known as *free electrons*. The electron has a negative electric charge, whereas the proton has a positive electric charge. The neutron has no net charge. Drawing electrons away from the atom causes it to have a net positive electric charge because of the excess of protons. The atom then attracts the negatively charged free electrons.

Some materials permit the movement of free electrons more easily than others. These materials are called *conductors*—copper, silver, and aluminum are good examples. Other materials restrict the movement of free electrons. These are called *insulators*, and glass, rubber, and air are examples of them.

The movement of electrons requires *energy*, which can be defined as the ability to perform work. A considerable amount of energy is needed to produce the flow of electricity which can be seen in the sparks that jump between oppositely charged materials. In Benjamin Franklin's famous experiment with a kite in a thunderstorm, he demonstrated that lightning was an electrical phenomenon involving an enormous amount of energy.

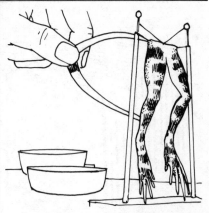

Franklin demonstrated that lightning is an electrical phenomenon.

Galvani noticed that two dissimilar pieces of metal caused a frog's leg to move.

Two Italians, Luigi Galvani and Alessandro Volta, made it possible to produce electricity in a form which could be used. Galvani discovered that a frog's leg could be made to twitch when it touched two dissimilar pieces of metal. Shortly afterwards, Volta showed that the movement in the frog's leg was caused by a flow of *current*, meaning a flow of free electrons. The current was produced by the electrochemical properties of the two pieces of metal. As a result, he was able to invent the Voltaic *cell*, a chemical method of generating electricity. The term *battery* is often used to designate a cell, but more accurately, a battery is a group of cells connected together to produce a greater amount of electricity. An automobile has a battery which contains a number of cells.

Volta's cell consisted of strips of two different metals that were placed in a solution of salt water. One of the metals was more chemically active than the other and gave off electrons, which were attracted by the less active metal. The two pieces of metal could be externally connected by a wire to create a *circuit*—a path through which an electric current passes. The more active metal became the negative *terminal* of the circuit, and the less active metal became the positive terminal.

Cells and batteries are still used as a source of electricity for many different purposes. A variety of metals and other substances are placed in solutions of salts, acids, or alkalis to make modern batteries. An automobile storage battery, for example, uses a solution of sulfuric

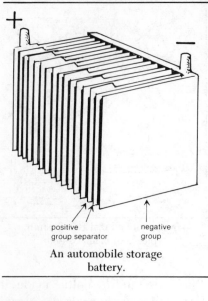

positive   negative
group separator   group

An automobile storage
battery.

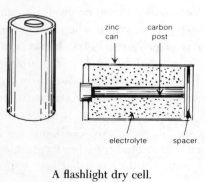

zinc   carbon
can   post

electrolyte   spacer

A flashlight dry cell.

acid in water with plates of lead and lead peroxide. A flashlight dry cell has a casing of zinc, the negative terminal, in which there is a paste of water and a salt called ammonium chloride. The positive terminal is a carbon strip placed inside the paste.

The two plates of the cell are called *electrodes*, and are placed in a solution known as the *electrolyte*. The positive plate is the *cathode*, and the negative is the *anode*. A problem that arises in the use of cells is a chemical reaction that deposits hydrogen bubbles on the anode, preventing electrons from passing into the electrode. In some kinds of cells the cathode will also gradually dissolve as a result of the continuous chemical reaction with the electrolyte. In storage batteries like those used in automobiles, the chemical reactions can be reversed by passing a reversed electric current through the electrolyte. This process is known as *recharging*, and it lengthens the life of the battery considerably.

The Voltaic cell opened up the way for the practical application of electricity, as we will see in the next unit. Chemical electricity is also widely used in the *electrolytic process*, or *electrolysis*. This process separates atoms that are combined in some molecules. A molecule is another tiny particle of matter which is made up of a combination of atoms. A molecule of water, for example, consists of two atoms of hydrogen and one of oxygen; a molecule of ordinary table salt is composed of one atom of sodium and one of chlorine.

When salt is dissolved, the chlorine atoms become negatively charged and the sodium atoms become positively charged because they have gained or lost electrons. Such electrically charged atomic particles are called *ions*. When electrodes are placed in the solution, the negatively charged chlorine ions collect at the anode, while the positively charged sodium ions collect at the cathode. There are other molecules which can be broken down into ionized atoms in solution. This is done by passing an electric current through the solution. This attracts ions of one element to the cathode and ions of the other to the anode.

The electrolytic process is used in refining aluminum from bauxite ore and in separating magnesium from chemicals found in sea water. It is also used for electroplating substances with metals such as silver and gold. Electrolysis is one of the most important processes available to chemists today.

Discussion

1. What phenomenon was observed by the Greek philosopher Thales more than two thousand years ago?

2. What did this phenomenon come to be called? How did it get its name?

3. What were two other discoveries that were made about static electricity after several hundred years?

4. What were the two kinds of electric charges called? How were they indicated?

5. What kinds of charges repel each other, and what kinds attract each other?

6. What was it learned actually causes electricity?

7. Describe the different parts of the atom and their relationship to each other.

8. Why is it possible to pull electrons away from the nucleus? What are electrons that remain in orbit called? What are those that have been pulled away from the nucleus called?

9. Why are free electrons attracted to atoms that have lost electrons?

10. What do conductors permit? What are some examples of good conductors?

11. What do insulators restrict? What are some good insulators?

12. What is the relationship between energy and the movement of free electrons? What are some familiar examples that show this relationship?

13. What did Luigi Galvani discover?

14. What caused the phenomenon observed by Galvani? Who made that discovery?

15. What was Volta able to invent? What is the difference between a cell and a battery?

16. What did Volta's cell consist of? What happened to the two metals in the cell?

17. What happened when a wire connected the two pieces of metal? Which became the negative terminal and which the positive terminal?

18. What are the materials in a modern automobile storage battery?

19. What are the materials in a modern flashlight dry cell?

20. What are the two plates of a cell called? Which is the anode and which is the cathode?

21. What is the solution in a cell called?

22. What are two problems that arise in the use of cells or batteries?

23. What can be done to lengthen the life of some kinds of cells or batteries?

24. How does electrolysis work?

25. What is a molecule? Give examples.

26. What happens to ordinary table salt when it is dissolved?

27. What is the name that is given to atoms that have lost or gained electrons to become electrically charged?

28. What happens when electrodes are placed in a salt water solution?

29. Is salt the only molecule that behaves in this way?

30. What minerals can be refined by electrolysis?

Review

A. Fill in the spaces in the following sentences with the appropriate word or phrase.

1. There are two kinds of electric charges, a _____ charge which is indicated by a _____ sign, and a _____ charge which is indicated by a _____ sign.

2. An electron is a subatomic particle that has a _____ electric charge.

3. A proton is a subatomic particle that has a _____ electric charge.

4. A neutron is a subatomic particle that has _____ electric charge.

5. _____ electricity can be produced by _____
_____, that is, by rubbing two different materials
together.

6. The atomic number of an element indicates the number of
_____ or _____ that the atom con-
tains.

7. _____ are materials that allow free electrons to
move through them easily.

8. _____ are materials that restrict the movement of
free electrons.

9. Electricity can perform work because the movement of free
electrons transmits _____.

10. When free electrons are flowing through a conductor, an electric _____ has been established.

11. In a cell the plates that become electrically charged are called
_____.

12. The _____ is an electrode with a negative
charge.

13. The _____ is an electrode with a positive
charge.

14. The solution of salt, acid, or alkali in which electrodes are
placed is called the _____.

15. An atom that has lost or gained electrons so that it is electrically charged is called an _____.

16. Like electric charges _____ each other and
unlike charges _____ each other.

17. Electrons that remain in orbit are known as _____ electrons, while those that have been pulled away from the atom are called _____ electrons.

B. Flashlights and automobiles are the only present-day uses of cells or batteries mentioned in the text. List some other common electrical devices which have cells or batteries as their source of electricity.

UNIT THREE
ELECTRIC CURRENTS AND
CIRCUITS

Special Terms

Electron Flow: The direction in which free electrons move through a conductor from the negative end to the positive end of a circuit. The term *current flow* is also used, but this dates from before the discovery of the electron, and in the nineteenth century was thought to indicate a flow of positive charges from the positive end to the negative end of a circuit.

Electromotive Force: The force or pressure that moves electrons through a conductor. It is abbreviated *emf.*

Volt: The unit of measurement of electromotive force. *Voltage* is the measurement of electromotive force expressed in volts. Volt is abbreviated *v.*

Ampere: The unit of measurement of the number of electrons flowing per second. *Amperage* is the measurement of the electron flow expressed in amperes. Ampere is abbreviated *amp.*

Resistance: The degree to which materials impede, or act against, the flow of electrons.

Ohm: The unit of measurement of resistance. It is sometimes abbreviated with the Greek letter omega (Ω).

Ohm's Law: A natural law that states the relationship between electromotive force, resistance, and rate of current flow. It can be expressed in a formula:

$$\text{Intensity (Amperage)} = \frac{\text{Voltage}}{\text{Resistance}}$$

Series Circuit: A circuit with only one path through which the current can flow.

Parallel Circuit: A circuit with two or more parallel paths through which an electric current can flow.

Series Parallel Circuit: A circuit that combines features of both series and parallel circuits.

Grounding: Connecting an electric circuit to the earth so that it is at the same voltage as the earth. This is often done for safety purposes. A *ground* is such a connection.

Fuse: A device to break an electric circuit when too much current is passing through it.

Short Circuit: A shortened path of current flow caused by zero resistance between two points on a circuit. It is usually due to defective wiring.

Direct Current: A steady flow of current in only one direction. It is abbreviated *dc*.

Alternating Current: A flow of current that reverses direction at regular intervals. It is abbreviated *ac*.

Watt: The unit of measurement of electric power, or energy per unit time.

Kilowatt: A thousand watts, abbreviated *kw*. A *megawatt* is a million watts.

Kilowatt Hour: The amount of energy consumed in one hour by an electrical device that uses energy at the rate of one kilowatt. It is abbreviated *kwh*. The kilowatt hour is the measurement that is ordinarily used in selling electric power.

Vocabulary Practice

1. What is the direction of *electron flow*? What other term is used? What did that term indicate in the nineteenth century?

2. What is *electromotive force*? How is it abbreviated?

3. What is a *volt*? How is it abbreviated?

4. What is an *ampere*? How is it abbreviated?

5. What is *resistance*?

6. What is an *ohm*? How is it sometimes abbreviated?

7. What is *Ohm's Law*? What is the formula that expresses it?

8. What is the difference between a *series circuit* and a *parallel circuit*?

9. What does a *series parallel circuit* combine?

10. What does *grounding* mean?

11. What is a *fuse* used for?

12. What is a *short circuit*? What usually causes it?

13. What is the difference between *direct current* and *alternating current*? How are they abbreviated?

14. What is a *watt*?

15. How many watts are there in a *kilowatt*? In a *megawatt*?

16. What is a *kilowatt hour*? How is it abbreviated? For what purpose is it usually used?

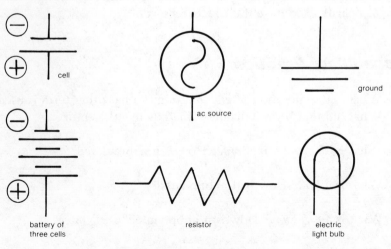

Symbols used for electric circuits.

Electric Currents and Circuits

An electric current is defined as the flow or movement of free electrons through a conductor. Because current can be both measured and controlled, it is a tremendously important source of energy in the modern world.

In the early days of experimentation with electricity, before the nature of the phenomenon was well understood, it was thought that electric current flowed in the same way as water. Thus, many terms referring to electricity are the same as those used to describe the movement of water. *Current flow* is one such term. We know now that electrons, which are negatively charged, flow externally through the circuit of a battery to the positive electrode. Formerly, however, it was believed that an electric current flowed in the opposite direction—from the positive to the negative side, just as water flows from full to empty. Because the term "current flow" was used to refer to this erroneous conception of electricity dominant in the nineteenth century, now the term *electron flow*, indicating the movement of electrons from the negative to the positive pole, is generally used instead.

The force that generates a flow of electricity is sometimes called pressure, like the pressure that causes water to flow. A more accurate term is *electromotive force*, usually abbreviated *emf*. The electromotive force is measured in *volts*, abbreviated with the letter *v*. Volts are named after the Italian scientist Alessandro Volta, mentioned in the previous unit.

The strength of a current, or the rate at which electrons move through a conductor, varies. The number of electrons flowing per second is measured in *amperes*, abbreviated *amp*. The ampere is named for a French scientist, André Ampère.

Different conductors allow the current to flow at different rates. The degree to which they impede, or act against, the flow of current is called *resistance*. Three excellent conductors of electricity are silver, copper, and aluminum. Silver has a lower resistance than copper, but copper is used for electric wires because it is cheaper than silver. As copper has become rarer and more expensive, however, aluminum has come into use for wiring purposes even though it has a slightly higher resistance than copper.

Resistance causes the electric energy to be changed into heat. An iron wire, for example, which has a higher resistance than copper or aluminum, will become red-hot when a strong enough current flows through it. Resistance is responsible for the heating and lighting effects of many common household appliances. In the electric light bulb a very thin wire (filament) of tungsten glows white-hot as current passes through it, thereby giving off light. Heating devices such as electric irons have resistors built in which heat up to the desired degree when a current moves through them.

Resistance is measured in *ohms*, sometimes abbreviated with the Greek letter omega (Ω). Ohms are named after a German scientist, Georg Simon Ohm.

Volts, amperes, and ohms can all be defined in numerical terms; that is, they can be quantified for use in arithmetical and mathematical calculations. The volt is defined as the electromotive force that sends one ampere of current through a resistance of one ohm. An ampere is defined as the number of electrons that pass through a point in one second. To give some idea of how tiny the electron is, the number per ampere is 6,280,000,000,000,000,000 electrons—more than six billion billion electrons. The ohm is defined as the resistance of a conductor that will permit one ampere of current to flow when a force of one volt has been applied.

The relation between these three measures of electric current can be stated in a formulation called *Ohm's Law*, which was first established by Georg Simon Ohm. Ohm's Law states that the current in an electric circuit varies directly according to the voltage and inversely (opposite) to the resistance. This is usually expressed in a formula:

$$I = \frac{E}{R}$$

I stands for the intensity of the current, or the amperage; *E* indicates the electromotive force, or the voltage; and *R* stands for the resistance. Thus, the formula is:

$$\text{Intensity (Amperage)} = \frac{\text{Electromotive Force (Voltage)}}{\text{Resistance}}$$

If the electromotive force is 120 volts and the resistance is 10 ohms, the voltage is divided by the resistance to determine the amperage:

$$120 \text{ volts} \div 10 \text{ ohms} = \text{Intensity} = 12 \text{ amperes}$$

The formula may be restated to find voltage or resistance:

$$E = IR$$

12 amperes $\times$ 10 ohms = Electromotive Force = 120 volts

$$R = \frac{E}{I}$$

120 volts $\div$ 12 amperes = Resistance = 10 ohms

    When a current has been generated, it flows in a path called a circuit. There are two basic kinds of circuits, depending on the way the electrical equipment is connected. The first is a *series circuit,* where the pieces of equipment are connected by wires that give the current only one path to follow.

    In the circuit diagram at the right, the symbol -W- indicates the source of electric current, and indicates the source of resistance—in this case a light bulb. The arrows indicate the electron flow from negative $(-)$ to positive $(+)$. This is the simplest type of series circuit, with only one resistor. The diagram below shows how two or more bulbs can be connected in a series circuit. A string of Christmas tree lights

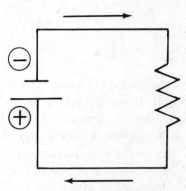

A simple series circuit.

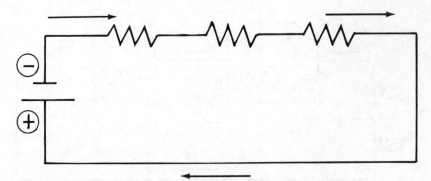

A series circuit with three resistors.

used to be a familiar example of a series circuit. Since the current had only one path to follow, all the lights in the circuit went out when even one bulb burned out.

The other basic type of circuit is called a *parallel circuit*. In this type of arrangement, two or more wires are placed parallel to each

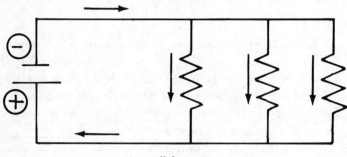

A parallel circuit.

other so that the current has more than one path through which it can flow. In the diagram above, the current is divided up among the three resistors. When the resistors in the circuit are light bulbs, if one burns out, current will continue to flow through the other two. Household electricity is connected by parallel circuits so that the whole circuit will not fail because of the failure of one piece of electrical equipment.

The two kinds of circuits can also be used together in a *series parallel circuit*. Two possible arrangements for series parallel circuits are shown in the diagrams below.

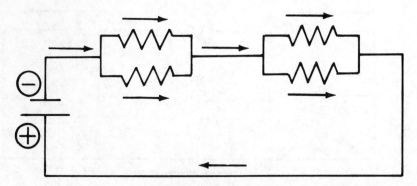

A series parallel circuit.

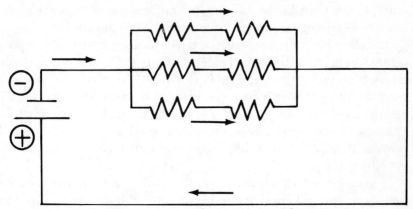

Another arrangement for a series parallel circuit.

The diagrams indicate that the circuit is completed by returning the wire to the positive terminal. In actual practice, many circuits and electrical appliances are *grounded* for safety reasons—one terminal, called the *ground*, is connected to the earth. This is done by connecting any metallic part of a machine or appliance to a water or sewer pipe. In case of electrical trouble, the current will go directly to the ground rather than through someone who accidentally touches the equipment. Dissolved salts in the earth provide positively charged ions that attract the free electrons.

When setting up a circuit, one must be sure that there is sufficient voltage to supply the current necessary to overcome the resistance. Thus, Ohm's Law not only has theoretical value but is also a useful and necessary tool for electrical engineers in their daily work.

When too many electrical appliances are placed in a circuit, the conducting wire may overheat. Therefore, most circuits are protected by *fuses* or other devices which break the circuit when it is overloaded. One familiar type of fuse has a wire with a low melting point protected by a window of a transparent mineral named mica. All the current in the circuit passes through the fuse. When the fuse heats up to a certain point at a specified rate of

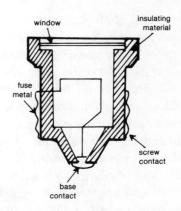

A household fuse.

current, the wire in the fuse melts and the circuit is broken. Most household circuits are wired for a current of 20 amperes.

A *short circuit* occurs when a zero resistance between two points on a wire shortens the path of electron flow. This usually results when the insulating material, the rubber or plastic covering the wire, has worn away so that two bare pieces of wire come into contact with each other. The current is simply following the path of least resistance. When a circuit overloads or shorts out, there is a hazard of fire. To prevent it, safety devices like fuses or circuit breakers must be built into the system.

There are two kinds of current flow, *direct current,* usually abbreviated *dc,* and *alternating current,* usually abbreviated *ac.* In direct current, the flow of electrons moves steadily in one direction. This is the kind of current that is generated by a flashlight cell or an automobile battery. In alternating current, the flow of electrons is reversed rapidly over and over again. This is called electromagnetism, and will be explained more fully in the next unit.

When Thomas Edison built the first generating station in New York in 1882, he supplied direct current for his system. After a long and bitter struggle, however, alternating current came into general use. Today it is used almost exclusively for homes and industry. The main advantage of alternating current is that there is less energy loss when current is transmitted over long distances.

Electric power can be expressed in another formula that is derived from Ohm's Law:

$$P = IE \text{ (Power = Intensity} \times \text{Electromotive Force)}$$

The unit of electric power is the *watt.* One watt is equal to a current of one ampere (the intensity) multiplied by one volt (the electromotive force). A current of 2 amperes and an electromotive force of 100 volts produces 200 watts of power.

The terms *kilowatt* and *megawatt* are also frequently used. A kilowatt is a thousand watts, and a megawatt is a million watts. The usual unit for measuring electric energy is the *kilowatt hour,* abbreviated *kwh,* the amount of energy used by a one-kilowatt electrical device operating for one hour. A 100-watt light bulb would use this amount of energy over a period of ten hours. The kilowatt hour is the unit which is ordinarily used in selling electric energy. Alternating current permits more efficient use of kilowatt hours. It enables the transmission of power at a high rate of voltage and a lower rate of current flow so that there is less heat and energy loss.

Discussion

1. What makes electric current such an important source of energy in the modern world?

2. Why are many of the terms used for electricity the same as those used for water?

3. Why is the term "electron flow" often used instead of "current flow?"

4. What terms are used for the force that generates a flow of electricity? What is the unit of measurement of this force? Who is it named for?

5. Does the current always flow through the conductor at the same rate? What is the unit of measurement for the number of electrons flowing per second? Who is the unit named for?

6. Do all conductors permit the current to flow at the same rate? Why not?

7. Why has copper been commonly used for electric wires? Why is aluminum now coming into wider use for that purpose?

8. How does resistance affect electric energy?

9. Give examples of how the property of resistance is used to produce heat and light in common household appliances.

10. What is the unit of measurement of resistance? How is it sometimes abbreviated? Who is it named for?

11. How are volts, amperes, and ohms defined in numerical terms?

12. What is the formula that expresses the relationship of the three measures of electricity? Give an example of finding the amperage when the voltage and resistance are known.

13. How can the formula be restated so that the voltage can be determined? Give an example of finding the voltage when the amperage and resistance are known.

14. How can the formula be restated to determine resistance? Give an example of finding the resistance when the voltage and amperage are known.

15. How are pieces of equipment connected in a series circuit?

16. What happens in a series circuit when one piece of equipment burns out?

17. How are pieces of equipment connected in a parallel circuit?

18. What happens when one piece of equipment burns out in a parallel circuit?

19. Why is household electricity connected by parallel circuits?

20. What is a third kind of electric circuit?

21. How can a circuit be grounded? Why is this done?

22. Why is Ohm's Law a useful and necessary tool for electrical engineers?

23. Why are circuits protected by fuses?

24. How does the common household fuse work?

25. What is a short circuit? What usually causes it?

26. Why are short circuits and overloaded circuits dangerous?

27. What are the two kinds of current? How are they different from each other?

28. What kind of current is generated by a cell or battery?

29. Which kind of current did Edison use for the first generating station in New York? Why is the other kind used almost exclusively now?

30. What is the formula by which electric power can be determined if the amperage and voltage are known?

31. What is the unit of electric power? What term is used for a thousand of these units? For a million of them?

32. How much electric energy is used in a kilowatt hour? How long would it take a 100-watt bulb to use a kilowatt hour?

33. How does alternating current permit more efficient transmission of electric energy?

Review

A. Find the intensity (amperage) with the information given:

1. 6 volts, 2 ohms

2. 220 volts, 10 ohms

3. 50 volts, 12.5 ohms

4. 120 volts, 20 ohms

5. 10 volts, 2 ohms

B. Find the electromotive force (voltage) with the information given:

   1. 10 amperes, 12 ohms

   2. 4 amperes, 7.5 ohms

   3. 20 amperes, 5 ohms

   4. 15 amperes, 7.5 ohms

   5. 2 amperes, 3 ohms

C. Find the resistance (ohms) with the information given:

   1. 110 volts, 10 amperes

   2. 10 volts, 5 amperes

   3. 60 volts, 30 amperes

   4. 60 volts, 20 amperes

   5. 125 volts, 12.5 amperes

D. Find the power (watts) with the information given:

   1. 2 amperes, 120 volts

   2. 2 amperes, 220 volts

   3. 10 amperes, 1,000 volts

   4. 20 amperes, 37,500 volts

   5. 12 amperes, 50,000 volts

E. Draw a diagram of a series circuit with 5 resistors.

F. Draw a diagram of a parallel circuit with 8 resistors.

G. Draw diagrams showing two possible arrangements for a series parallel circuit with 8 resistors.

UNIT FOUR
ELECTROMAGNETISM

Special Terms

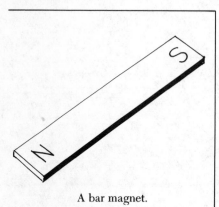

A bar magnet.

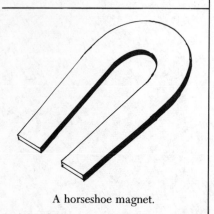

A horseshoe magnet.

Magnet: An object which has the property of attracting iron and certain other materials. The property itself is called *magnetism.*

North Pole/South Pole: The two ends of a magnet, where the force of magnetism is strongest. Like poles repel each other and unlike poles attract each other.

Magnetic Field: The entire area in which a magnet exerts its force.

Lines of Force: Lines showing the direction and strength of the forces exerted within a magnetic field.

Electromagnetism: The magnetic force exerted by an electric current.

Coil: An electric wire twisted into a spiral shape.

Armature: A magnetized metal bar used in electric motors.

Commutator: A device used in electric motors to reverse the flow of current.

Stator: The stationary part of an electric motor or generator.

Rotor: The rotating part of an electric motor or generator.

Generator: A machine for generating electromotive force (voltage). The term usually applies to machines that generate electricity by means of electromagnetism.

A coil around an iron core.

Turbine: A device with blades moved by water or steam. The turbine turns the rotor in an electric generator.

Transformer: A device for increasing or decreasing the voltage of alternating current. A *step-up transformer* increases voltage, and a *step-down transformer* decreases it.

Primary Coil/Secondary Coil: The two coils of a transformer. Alternating current enters through the primary coil and produces an increased or decreased voltage in the secondary coil.

Vocabulary Practice

1. What is a *magnet*? What is the name of the property possessed by magnets?

2. What are the *north* and *south poles* of a magnet? Which poles attract, and which repel each other?

3. What is a *magnetic field*?

4. What are *lines of force*?

5. What is *electromagnetism*?

6. What is a *coil*?

7. What is an *armature*?

8. What is a *commutator*?

9. What is the difference between a *stator* and a *rotor*?

10. What is a *generator*?

11. What is the relation of a *turbine* to a generator?

12. What is the difference between a *step-up* and a *step-down transformer*?

13. Through which coil does current enter a transformer and what effect is produced?

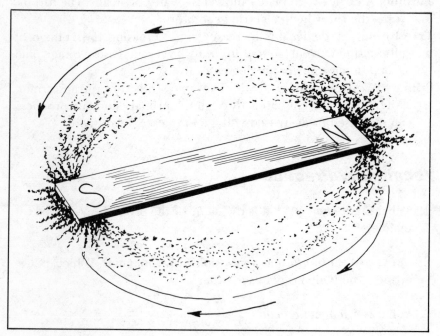

The lines of force of a magnetic field.

Electromagnetism

In addition to static electricity, the ancient Greeks observed another natural phenomenon. They discovered a kind of iron ore which possessed the ability to attract or repel certain other kinds of material, especially iron. This property is called *magnetism*, and an object that possesses it is called a *magnet*. Iron containing a small amount of carbon can be made into a magnet by placing it in contact with another magnet; it is then said to have been magnetized.

When two bar magnets are brought together, one end of the first magnet attracts one end of the second magnet, but repels the opposite end of that magnet. If the direction of one magnet is reversed, the attraction and repulsion are also reversed. The two ends of a magnet are called *north* and *south poles*, shortened forms for "north-seeking" and "south-seeking" poles, because when a magnet is allowed to pivot freely, one end always points toward the north and the other end toward the south. This is because the earth itself is a giant magnet with magnetic poles near the geographic North and South Poles.

A magnet does not simply exert a force of attraction in a straight line from one pole to the other. Rather, it establishes a *magnetic field*, in which the direction and strength of the force are indicated by *lines of force*. These extend out from each pole of the magnet and meet to form an oval-shaped arc. Lines of force go out of the north pole and back into the south pole. Where the magnetic field is strongest there are proportionately more lines of force.

There is an obvious similarity between the phenomena of electricity and magnetism. We have already noted that like electric charges repel and unlike charges attract. With magnets, like poles repel and unlike poles attract.

The relationship between electricity and magnetism was discovered accidentally by a Danish scientist, Hans Oersted, in 1819. He had left a compass on a table where he was experimenting with an electric current. A compass is a navigational device with a magnetized needle which points to the earth's north and south magnetic poles. Oersted observed that the needle moved whenever the current was turned on, and concluded that electric current possessed the property of magnetism. Oersted had discovered the phenomenon of *electromagnetism*, a discovery which has had momentous conse-

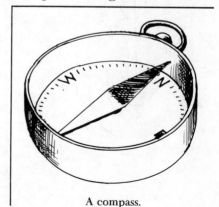

A compass.

quences. It has led to the development of many devices which make use of electromagnetism, including electric motors, generators, and transformers. Without these devices, electricity could never have become a major source of power.

Other scientists experimenting with electromagnetism found that the magnetic effect of an electric current could be strengthened by sending the current through a *coil*—a wire conductor twisted into a spiral shape. A greater number of turns of wire in the coil strengthens the magnetism, as does a stronger electric current. Wrapping the coil around a core of iron further increases the magnetism, because the iron itself becomes magnetized. All these discoveries led the way to converting electromagnetic energy into motion. The great advantage of this energy conversion is that devices based on electromagnetism can be controlled simply by switching the current on or off.

One such device is an electric motor, in which a bar known as an *armature* is placed between the two arms of a horseshoe magnet. Magnetic poles are induced in the armature by sending a current through a coil wrapped around it. Magnetic force then causes it to move in the direction in which the unlike poles attract each other. Of course, if the poles of the armature reached a position directly opposite the unlike poles of the horseshoe magnet, the armature would become locked and no further motion would be possible. It is necessary, therefore, to prevent the unlike poles from becoming aligned. In a direct current electric motor, this is done by a device called a *commutator*, which reverses the electron flow, changing the magnetic poles of the armature at each half-turn. This causes the armature to move on to the new poles of

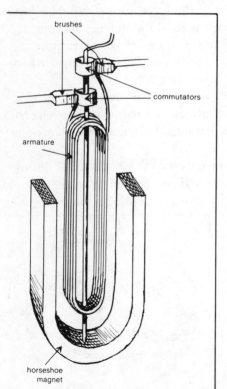

brushes

commutators

armature

horseshoe
magnet

A dc electric motor.

attraction, completing a full rotation, or "cycle."

In an alternating current electric motor, the stationary portion is called a *stator* and the rotating portion, a *rotor*. With alternating current, the flow of electrons reverses at rapid intervals. The intervals are timed to change the stator and rotor poles simultaneously so that the rotor continues to move in a circle, or cycle. In the United States, alternating current electric motors are timed to complete 60 cycles per second (abbreviated cps), but in Europe they are timed for 50 cycles per second.

The property of electromagnetism is also vital to the production of electrical power. Electricity from chemical action—the cell or battery—is suitable only for special and limited uses. *Generators* based on electromagnetism, however, produce sufficient cheap electricity to supply most of the world's needs.

Not long after the discovery that a magnetic field could be created by an electric current, the English scientist Michael Faraday

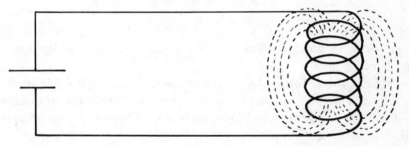

A loop of wire passing through a magnetic field.

discovered that the reverse was also true—a current could be created by a magnetic field. When a closed loop of wire moves through a magnetic field, an electromotive force is created. This causes a current of electrons to flow through the wire and is the basis for generating electricity. Because it is electromotive force that is produced, the power of generators is described in terms of volts, the units of measurement for emf. To generate emf, the wire must cut the lines of force in the magnetic field; if the wire moves parallel to them, no emf is produced. Also, the faster the wires are made to move, the greater the production of emf. For this reason, a rotary (circular) motion is used in a generator rather than a reciprocating (up-and-down or back-

and-forth) motion—it is much easier to maintain a rotary motion at high speeds.

A generator contains a stator, a stationary magnet, with a rotor placed between its north and south poles. As the rotor turns, the wires in it cut the lines of force in the magnetic field of the stator. With each

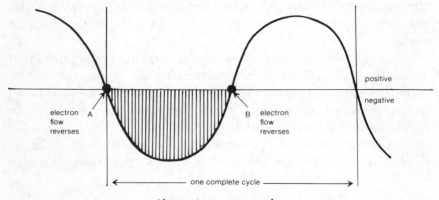

positive

negative

electron flow reverses A

B electron flow reverses

one complete cycle

Alternating current cycle.

half-turn the current flow is reversed. This is what produces alternating current, in which the electron flow rapidly changes direction over and over again.

The rotor is turned by a *turbine*, a machine with huge blades which are generally moved by water or steam. Steam for an electric power plant can be obtained from the heat supplied by burning coal or oil, or by nuclear fission.

The enormous size of modern generators and the speed with which the rotor can turn mean that electric power of very high voltage can be produced. As much as half a million volts can be transmitted over high-voltage lines to substations. There the voltage is reduced to strengths that can be used in factories or homes. In the United States the customary voltage for household use has become 110-120v, since it was discovered that higher voltages could cause fatal accidents. 220v is still supplied for some heavy-duty uses, however, such as for operating an electric stove.

Transformers are the devices that increase or decrease the amount of voltage. Like generators, they also depend on electromagnetic effects.

A transformer basically consists of two coils of wire wrapped around iron cores. Current is supplied to a transformer through the

A turbine and generator. (Courtesy of Con Edison,
New York)

primary coil and is taken from the *secondary coil.* When an alternating
current passes through the primary coil, the constant reversal of electron flow produces a changing magnetic field that creates a current in
the secondary coil.

When the primary coil has more turns than the secondary coil,
the secondary voltage is decreased; this is a *step-down transformer.*
When the secondary coil has more turns than the primary, the secondary voltage is increased; this is a *step-up transformer.* Step-up transformers are used at a power plant to increase the voltage for transmission. As we have pointed out, the higher the voltage in transmission,
the less energy loss takes place. At substations that distribute electricity for use, and in all buildings or houses supplied with electricity,
there are step-down transformers to change the power to voltages
suitable for industrial or domestic use.

A modern transformer at a 4000-kilovolt substation
in New Mexico. (Courtesy of
New Mexico Electric Service Company)

Discussion

1. What did the Greeks observe about a certain kind of iron ore? What is this phenomenon called?

2. What can be done to iron containing carbon?

3. What happens when two bar magnets are brought together?

4. What are the names for the ends of a magnet? Why were they given these names?

5. In what direction does magnetism exert a force of attraction?

6. What is an important similarity between magnetism and electricity?

7. Who discovered electromagnetism? How did he discover it?

8. What is a compass?

9. Why was Oersted's discovery of such great importance?

10. What other discoveries were made about electromagnetism?

11. What is the great advantage of converting electromagnetic energy into motion?

12. What is the name of the bar in an electric motor? Where is it placed?

13. What happens when an electric current flows through the coil around the armature?

14. Why is it necessary to prevent the unlike poles from becoming aligned? How is this prevented in a direct current motor?

15. What are the names of the two main parts of an alternating current electric motor?

16. Why is the rotor able to continue moving in a complete circle?

17. How are ac electric motors timed in the United States? In Europe?

18. What discovery made it possible to generate electricity by means of electromagnetism? What happens when a loop of wire is passed through a magnetic field?

19. Why is the power of generators described in terms of volts?

20. Why is a rotary motion better for producing electricity than a reciprocating motion?

21. How is alternating current produced by a generator?

22. What turns the rotor in a generator? Where does the power come from?

23. Is electricity transmitted at low or high voltages?

24. Why has 110-120v come into common use for households in the United States? Is any other voltage in use?

25. What do transformers do?

26. What are the basic parts of a transformer?

27. Through which coil is current supplied to a transformer? From which is the current taken?

28. What happens when the primary coil has more turns than the secondary? What kind of transformer is this?

29. What happens when the secondary coil has more turns than the primary? What kind of transformer is this?

30. Why are step-up transformers used at power plants?

31. Why are step-down transformers used at distribution sub-stations?

Review

A. Fill in the spaces in the following sentences with the appropriate word or phrase.

1. The ancient Greeks discovered that certain kinds of _____ ore could attract or repel other substances. They called this phenomenon _____.

2. The two ends of a magnet are called the _____ and the _____.

3. A _____ is used for navigation because its magnetized needle points in the directions of the geographic
_____ and _____.

4. Like poles of a magnet _____, and unlike poles
_____.

5. The _____ extending out from a magnet are
_____ in shape. They indicate the
_____ established by the magnet.

6. A generator creates an electromotive force which is expressed
in terms of _____.

7. Electromagnetism can be increased by winding a
_____ of conducting wire around an iron core.

8. In an electric motor, a bar known as an _____ is
placed between the arms of a horseshoe magnet.

9. A _____ in an electric motor changes the direction of the electron flow so that the armature continues to
move.

10. A _____ motion is circular and a
_____ motion is back-and-forth or up-and-down.

11. Current enters a transformer through the _____
coil and is taken from the _____ coil.

12. A transformer that increases voltage is a _____
transformer; one that decreases voltage is a _____
transformer.

13. A _____ is the moving part of a generator and a
_____ is the stationary part.

14. The moving part of a generator is turned by a
_____ which is usually powered by
_____ or _____.

15. There is less energy loss when electricity is transmitted at a high _____.

B. Indicate the north pole and the south pole of the magnet in the drawing below.

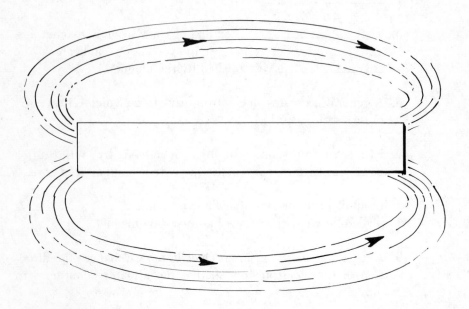

C. Indicate in which direction these magnetizable particles would point if the north pole of a magnet were placed in the position on the left.

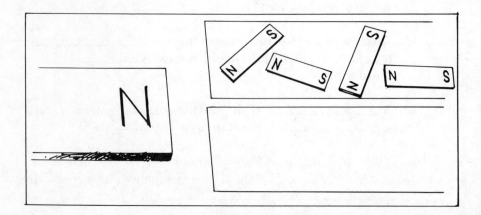

D. Indicate in which direction these magnetizable particles would
   point if the south pole of a magnet were placed in the position on
   the left.

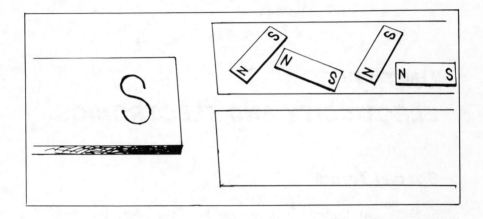

UNIT FIVE
ELECTRICITY AND ELECTRONICS

Special Terms

Incandescent Light: Light produced by the white-hot glow of a heated substance. The common electric light bulb gets its incandescence from a white-hot filament of tungsten.

Corpuscle: A small particle; it was the name first given to what we now call the electron.

Vacuum: A space from which matter, including air, has been removed. A light bulb contains a partial vacuum.

Semiconductor: A substance with a higher degree of resistance than good conductors like copper, but a lower resistance than insulators like rubber.

Radio Waves: Electromagnetic waves produced by the oscillation, or vibration, of electric charges. They are used for communication by radio.

Atomic Fission: Splitting the nucleus of an atom, thereby releasing energy. It is also called *nuclear fission.* Present-day nuclear energy is based on fission.

Atomic Fusion: Joining the nuclei of atoms with a resulting release of energy. It is called *nuclear fusion.* As a source of energy, this is presently in the experimental stage.

Kilovolt: A thousand volts.

Rectifier: A device which changes alternating current to direct current.

Kinetic Energy: Energy that comes from motion, such as the motion of water that turns a turbine in an electric power plant.

Piezoelectricity: Electricity that comes from pressure or weight applied to certain crystals.

Thermoelectricity: Electricity that comes from heat applied to a *thermocouple*, a joint of two different metals.

Photoelectricity: The release of electrons with a resulting electromotive force caused by the effect of light on some substances.

Vocabulary Practice

1. What is *incandescent light*? What causes the incandescence of the common electric light bulb?

2. What is a *corpuscle*? What was the term once used to describe?

3. What is a *vacuum*?

4. What is a *semiconductor*?

5. What are *radio waves*?

6. What is the difference between *atomic fission* and *atomic fusion*? Which one is a practical source of energy now?

7. How many volts are there in a *kilovolt*?

8. What is a *rectifier*?

9. What is *kinetic energy*? Give two examples of kinetic energy.

10. What is *piezoelectricity*?

11. What is *thermoelectricity*?

12. What is *photoelectricity*?

13. What are the other sources of electricity that have been discussed up to this point?

A 765,000-volt transmission line of the American Electric Power System, capable of carrying 30 times as much power as the 138,000-volt lines standard throughout much of the United States. (Courtesy of American Electric Power Service Corporation)

Electricity and Electronics

Volta made his experimental cell in 1800, producing for the first time a steady, reliable electric current. During the nineteenth century, the development of practical applications of electrical energy advanced rapidly. The first major uses of electricity were in the field of communications—first for the telegraph and then the telephone. They used not only electric current but also electromagnetic effects.

Thomas Edison's invention of the electric light bulb, based on *incandescent light,* was perhaps the most momentous development of all, but not because it was such a unique invention. Actually, other people were working simultaneously on the same technical problem, and Edison's claim to the invention was disputed. It was momentous because it led to the creation of an electric power system which has since reached into nearly every corner of the world. Perhaps Edison's most important claim to fame is his pioneering work in engineering, which helped to provide electric service for New York City in 1882.

The applications of electricity have grown to the point where most of us lead "electrified lives," surrounded by a variety of devices that use electric energy. Less visible, but probably more important, are the thousands of ways industry has put electric energy to work.

It is quite remarkable that so much of this rapid development of electrical devices and the resulting industry took place during the nineteenth century, when the nature of electricity was not completely understood. We have already observed that for a long time, it was incorrectly believed that current flowed from positive to negative. It was not until 1897 that the British scientist Sir Joseph Thomson published a paper announcing his discovery of a subatomic particle, the electron (first called a *corpuscle*). Up to that time it had been generally believed that the atom was an indivisible particle of matter.

Thomson's discovery led to further experimentation into the structure of the atom. He may be considered the founder of the modern science of nuclear physics. Within the field of electricity, his work led to the creation of the science of electronics. There is so much confusion in current usage between the terms "electricity" and "electronics" that we should attempt to make some sort of distinction between them.

Electricity generally refers to the flow of free electrons through a conductor, in other words, to a current of electricity. The term includes the electric power supplied by generators and the distribution systems which transmit it to homes, offices, and factories.

Electronics, on the other hand, deals with the movement of free electrons in a *vacuum* or in *semiconductors*. When the term first came into use, it referred to the behavior of free electrons in vacuum tubes like those used to transmit or detect *radio waves*. Since then it has been extended to include the movement of electrons in gases, liquids, and solids which had not previously been considered to be conductors.

Electronic refinements have greatly extended the uses and capabilities of some of the older electrical devices. The switching devices necessary for the direct dialing of telephone calls are the result of electronic engineering. As we shall see in Unit Seven, the transistor, an invention which has revolutionized the science of electronics, was first developed for use in telephone equipment.

Regardless of the distinction made between the two fields, both must be understood by today's electrical and electronic engineers. Even an engineer working on the design of the newest computer must have a knowledge of circuits and electromagnetic effects. Electricity and electronics are really indivisible; each one forms part of the other.

There has been so much emphasis on electronic developments— and so much publicity given them—that until recently they seemed to have taken over the electrical and electronic field completely. The general attitude was that electric power systems had already advanced as far as they could, and that anything new and exciting would come from the area of electronics. However, the current shortage of energy sources throughout the world has shown that there is still a need for research and development in the field of electricity. This need exists primarily in three areas: improving present systems of generating and transmitting electric power, discovering practicable new systems for generating electric power, and creating systems to derive electricity from new sources.

We have noted that most electricity is generated by powerful electromagnetic devices turned by turbines that use water or steam as a source of power. In recent years, however, nuclear energy derived from *atomic fission*, the splitting of the nuclei of atoms, has become more important. Research also continues into *nuclear fusion*, the joining together of atomic nuclei with a great release of energy. Finding a way to exploit this source of power would be a tremendous advance, since the fuel for fusion would consist principally of molecules that occur in water. Research of this kind is typically done by teams of scientists and engineers from a variety of different disciplines.

In order to reduce energy loss in the transmission of electricity, researchers are looking for methods of transmitting increasingly high voltages. Transmission lines that will carry a million volts are presently under development. Systems for increasing the efficiency of transmitting direct current electricity have already been introduced. A direct current submarine line carrying 100 *kilovolts* (100,000 volts: a kilovolt equals a thousand volts) was put into operation in Sweden in 1954. The transmission of high-voltage direct current depends on an electronic device called a *rectifier,* which changes alternating current to direct current.

Researchers are also trying to develop new systems of

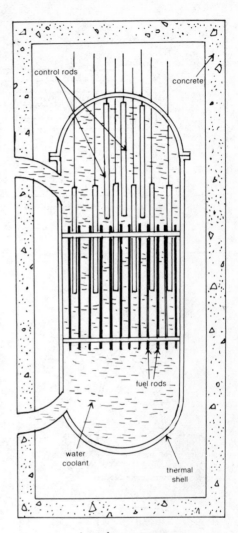

A nuclear reactor.

generating electricity, some of which involve new sources of energy. One part of this research has concentrated on finding a new source of power to drive the turbine, such as the *kinetic energy* (energy that comes from motion) of the wind and tides. Another line of research attempts to develop other known but so far impracticable methods for generating electricity. These include *piezoelectricity—* electricity that comes from pressure or weight applied to certain kinds of crystals. More promising is *thermoelectricity,* or the generation of electricity through heat. When the joint between two dif-

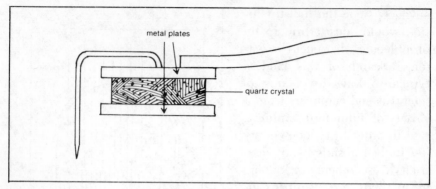

metal plates

quartz crystal

An example of piezoelectricity.

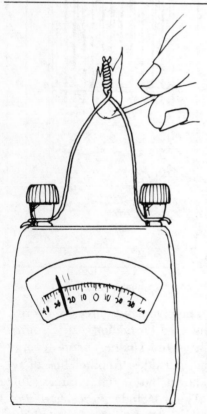

A heated thermocouple produces
electromotive force.

ferent metals is heated, a weak electromotive force is created. The joint is called a *thermocouple*, and several thermocouples joined in a series, like cells in a battery, increase the electromotive force. Thermoelectric generators, with heat supplied from radioactive materials, have been used in equipment for the space program. The action of light on some substances can also produce a release of electrons with an electromotive force. This effect is known as *photoelectricity*. It is familiar to most of us in the photoelectric cells that open and close automatic doors when a beam of light is broken.

Finally, attempts are being made to improve the means of producing electricity from chemical reactions in cells and batteries. Although electric cars powered by batteries have existed for a long time, they still cannot compete with cars powered by internal combustion engines, which burn increasingly scarce and expensive gasoline. There have been some promising discoveries in battery research, however, which may hasten the development of a practical battery-powered car. An electric car produced at a low enough price and with a long enough operation time would offer two advantages over the internal combustion engine: it would save fuel and avoid further pollution of the atmosphere.

Discussion

1. What opened up the way for practical applications of electricity?

2. What were the first major uses of electricity?

3. Why was Edison's invention of the incandescent light bulb a momentous development in the field of electricity?

4. What may be Edison's most lasting claim to fame?

5. How has electricity changed our lives?

6. Why was the rapid development of electrical devices during the nineteenth century so remarkable?

7. What discovery did Sir Joseph Thomson announce in 1897? What had generally been believed up till then?

8. What two new sciences is Thomson considered to have founded?

9. What does the term "electricity" usually refer to nowadays?

10. What does electronics deal with?

11. What did the term "electronics" refer to when it first came into use? What has it been extended to include?

12. What has happened to some of the older electrical devices? Give an example.

13. Why must an electrical or electronic engineer today understand both these areas?

14. What attitude about the field of electricity existed until recently?

15. Why has this attitude changed?

16. In what three areas of the field of electricity does a need exist for research and development?

17. How is most electricity generated?

18. What new source of energy has become important in recent years?

19. What would be the advantage of energy from nuclear fusion?

20. Are only electrical and electronic engineers doing research into nuclear fusion?

21. What developments are taking place in the transmission of electricity?

22. What device is necessary for the transmission of high voltage direct current?

23. What new sources of power could be used to drive the turbine?

24. What is the name for electricity that comes from pressure applied to certain crystals?

25. Does thermoelectricity create a strong or weak electromotive force? How can the force be strengthened?

26. Where have thermoelectric generators been used?

27. How is photoelectricity produced?

28. What is a familiar example of the use of photoelectricity?

29. What is being done to improve electric cars?

30. What advantages would electric cars have over those with internal combustion engines?

Review

Write a short composition about possible new ways to generate electric power. You should discuss ways of improving present systems, possibilities for developing new systems, and possible new sources of energy.

UNIT SIX
RADIO WAVES AND VACUUM TUBES

Special Terms

Electromagnetic Waves: Waves produced when a regular disturbance in an electromagnetic field causes an electric charge to oscillate. These waves travel at the speed of light. The kind used in radio transmission are called *radio waves*.

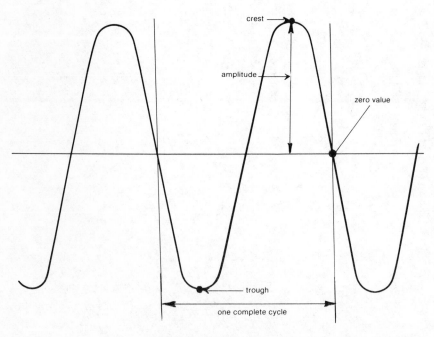

Electromagnetic waves.

Oscillate: To vibrate, or swing back and forth between two extreme points.

Amplitude: The height of a wave from the point of equilibrium, or *zero value*, to the *crest.*

Frequency: The number of wave cycles produced per second.

Oscillator: A device for generating electromagnetic waves.

Modulation: The process of modulating, or varying, radio waves according to electrical signals generated by sound waves, in order to transmit sound. There are two types of modulation: *amplitude modulation*, abbreviated *AM*, in which the height, or amplitude, of the wave is changed; and *frequency modulation*, abbreviated *FM*, in which the number of cycles per second is varied.

Amplifier: A device used to amplify, or strengthen, radio, sound, or light waves.

Vacuum Tube: A tube from which air and other matter have been removed. Electrons are able to flow across the space in the tube from the cathode (negative electrode) to the anode (positive electrode).

High Vacuum: A vacuum which is closer to a complete vacuum than the partial vacuum in most tubes.

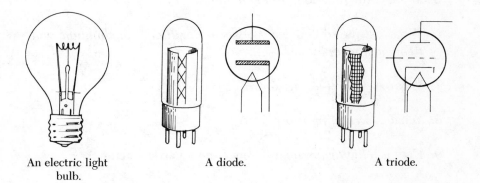

An electric light   A diode.   A triode.
bulb.

Diode: A vacuum tube containing a cathode and an anode that are not internally connected by a conductor.

Triode: A vacuum tube with a cathode, an anode, and a third electrode called a *grid.*

Phototube: A tube in which electrons are released by the energy of light.

Image Orthicon Tube: A special electronic tube that picks up light images and converts them into electrical signals for transmission. It is the basis for television.

Radar: An electronic system for locating aircraft or cloud patterns by interpreting the echoes of very high frequency radio waves.

Sonar: An underwater navigation system consisting of electronic devices which detect sound wave echoes.

Vocabulary Practice

1. What are *electromagnetic waves?*

2. What is the *amplitude* of a wave?

3. What is the *frequency* of a wave?

4. What does an *oscillator* do?

5. What is the function of *modulation?*

6. What is the difference between *amplitude modulation* and *frequency modulation?*

7. What are *amplifiers* used for?

8. What is a *vacuum tube?*

9. How is a *high vacuum* different from a partial vacuum?

10. What is the difference between a *diode* and a *triode?*

11. How do both a diode and triode differ from an ordinary electric light bulb?

12. What is a *phototube?*

13. What is the function of an *image orthicon tube?*

14. What is *radar?*

15. What is *sonar?*

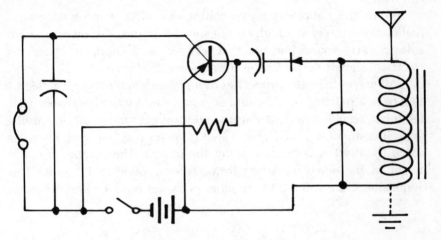

Diagram of a radio system.

Radio Waves and Vacuum Tubes

In 1865 the English scientist James Maxwell predicted that *electromagnetic waves* would be produced if an electric charge were made to *oscillate,* or vibrate back and forth. These waves would travel at the speed of light, 186,000 miles per second. In 1887 a German scientist, Heinrich Hertz, actually produced and measured such waves, the kind we now call *radio waves.* By 1901 the Italian inventor Guglielmo Marconi had succeeded in sending a signal across the Atlantic by means of electromagnetic waves. The way was now open for the radio, which could transmit sound over long distances without the use of wires. In fact, the radio was often called the "wireless" in its early days, a term still used in England.

Communication by electrical signals had already been achieved with the telegraph and the telephone, but both devices required the use of a conducting wire. The telegraph sends a coded message over the wire in the form of electrical signals, which are produced by making and breaking the electric circuit at specified intervals. A receiver converts the signals into sounds which are then decoded. A telephone actually transmits sound. Sound is produced by vibrations which cause disturbances in the air known as sound waves. The telephone converts these sound waves into vibrating electrical signals that are carried over the wire and then converted back into sound by a receiver.

With the radio, expensive cables and wires were unnecessary. Radio waves travel at a high rate of speed over long distances, and are able to carry sound because they can be modulated, or varied, by electrical signals derived from the slower sound waves.

All waves have the properties of *amplitude* and *frequency*. Beginning from a point of equilibrium, or *zero value*, a wave fluctuates back and forth, reaching two extremes; on returning to the point of equilibrium, it completes a full cycle. The high point reached by the wave is called the *crest*, and the low point, the trough. The amplitude is the height of the wave measured from its zero value to its crest. The frequency of the wave is the number of cycles produced per second.

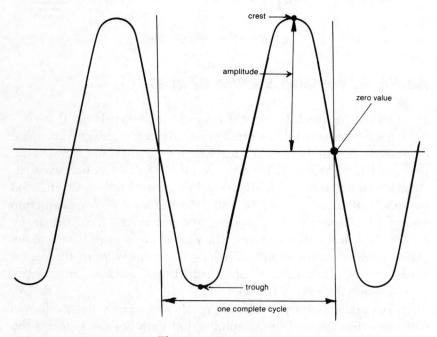

Electromagnetic waves.

In radio, an *oscillator* produces vibrations which send out electromagnetic waves. Sound waves are converted into electrical vibrations which are used to adapt, or modulate, these waves. There are two types of *modulation: amplitude modulation (AM)*, in which the amplitude of the "carrier" wave is changed by the sound-generated electrical wave; and *frequency modulation (FM)*, in which the frequency of the carrier wave is changed.

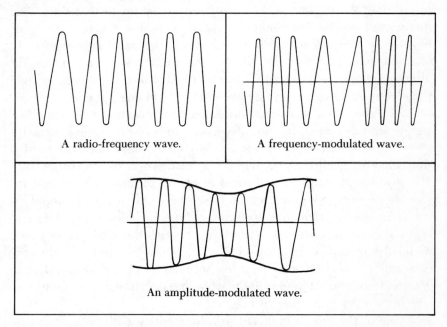

A radio-frequency wave.

A frequency-modulated wave.

An amplitude-modulated wave.

To produce a working radio it was necessary to develop many special devices—oscillators to produce waves, *amplifiers* to strengthen them, and rectifiers to change alternating to direct current. It was in developing these devices that the science now called electronics made its first contribution: the *vacuum tube*. Placed at certain points in the circuit of the radio, vacuum tubes performed several different functions by controlling the flow of electricity in much the same way as valves control the flow of liquids and gases.

A vacuum is a space from which matter has been removed. As we have seen, there is a partial vacuum within the electric light bulb. Current flows through the resistance of a filament of tungsten placed in the vacuum, causing the filament to become white-hot, and thereby give off light. Even before the invention of the incandescent lamp, an English scientist named William Crookes had experimented with a vacuum tube that glowed under special circumstances. Edison also had observed what is known as the "Edison effect"—a flow of electricity across a vacuum from the cathode to the anode without the presence of a conductor. These observations were among those that led to Thomson's discovery of the electron. By 1904 another English scientist, John Ambrose Fleming, had invented a vacuum tube, now called a *diode*, that could be used to detect radio signals more accurately than the crystals which had been in use up to that time. The diode contained a hot filament and a plate; the filament gave off negatively charged electrons, which were attracted to the positively charged plate. When the diode was placed in a circuit using alternating current, the current was rectified to direct current, because the electrons flowed across the vacuum only in one direction.

In 1906 Lee De Forest, an American inventor, made another significant advance in the use of vacuum tubes when he invented the *triode*. In addition to a cathode and an anode, the triode contained a third electrode called a *grid*, which was placed between the other two. The grid could control the flow of electrons through the vacuum by varying its voltage with respect to the cathode. Many further improvements in the vacuum tube followed. These included using different types of gases to achieve special effects, coating the inside of the tubes with substances that gave off light when struck by electrons (fluorescent tubes), creating *high vacuum* tubes through the removal of a greater amount of air and other matter, and developing vacuum tubes which used the properties of magnetism.

One of the most significant developments was the *phototube*, in which electrons are released by the action of light on a photosensitive

An automatic garage door opens as a car breaks a beam of light.

surface. Since phototubes give off a very weak current, they are used with amplifiers which increase the strength of the electron flow. One of the most familiar uses of phototubes is for doors that open or close automatically when a beam of light is broken. Phototubes are often used in security systems, and also have many industrial applications.

A more important use of photoelectric effects has been to create television. The key element in a television system is an *image orthicon tube.* At one end of the tube is a light sensitive screen on which an image is focused by a camera. Since brighter spots of light release more electrons, when the electrons strike a "target" screen in the tube, they reproduce the image in the form of thousands of spots of light of varying brightness. At the other end of the tube is an electron gun that scans these dots of light at a high rate of speed. As the electrons bounce off the target screen, they are converted into electromagnetic waves which transmit the image to receivers.

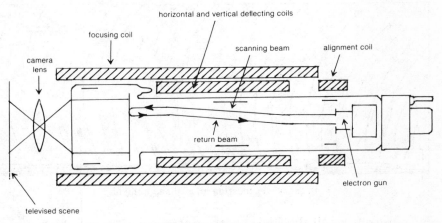

An image orthicon tube.

In the television receiver is another tube that interprets these electronic signals and projects them onto the screen of the set. The screen is coated with fluorescent materials that react to the signals by giving off light of the same intensity, or brightness, as the original image. The picture on the screen is made up of thousands of tiny dots of differing degrees of intensity, similar to those you would see if you looked at a newspaper picture through a magnifying glass.

In color television, three image orthicon tubes are used, one each for green, red, and blue light. In the picture tube of the receiver there are three separate electron beams that project the image onto the screen. The screen has thousands of separate dots sensitive to each color, arranged in triangular groups.

The vacuum tube created many new applications for electronics. It is not possible to discuss all of them here, but it is worthwhile to mention two of the most important, *radar* and *sonar*. Radar is used for locating aircraft, and sonar for locating underwater obstructions and measuring depth. They both take advantage of the echo property of waves—waves are reflected back when they strike an obstruction or barrier of some kind. In radar, radio waves are reflected back from aircraft in flight. Radio waves, as we have noted, travel at the speed of light, 186,000 miles per second, and the echo is also returned at extremely high speeds. To make radar a reality, electronic devices were developed that could distinguish between different waves with an interval between them of only a microsecond—a millionth of a second!

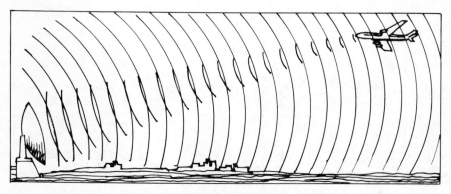

Radar waves locating an airplane in flight.

In spite of all the advances that were made, vacuum tubes presented certain difficulties which made them unsatisfactory for use in many electronic devices, such as the computer. First, they needed time to warm up. Although the time in some cases was only a fraction of a second, it could cause operational problems. Second, vacuum tubes occupied a lot of space even after technological improvements had reduced them in size. Though early computers were constructed with vacuum tubes, in the more complex computers used today they would occupy so much space that an entire building would be necessary to house the equipment. Such a computer would also need hundreds of miles of electric wiring to connect all the tubes. Third, they were not reliable, because the tubes might burn out, just as electric light bulbs burn out after they have been in use for a period of time. In fact, it is hard to imagine that computers using only vacuum tubes were ever in perfect working order, with every single tube functioning properly at the same time. Finally, the tubes gave off a great deal of heat. This increased the amount of room necessary for them, since space had to be left between them for air to circulate and cool them. In some cases, the heat itself could cause problems in the operation of the device.

All of these problems led to the search for a device that would perform the same function as the vacuum tube without presenting so many difficulties. With the invention of the transistor, electronics entered a new phase, which we will discuss in the next unit.

Discussion

1. What was predicted by the English scientist James Maxwell in 1865?

2. When and by whom were electromagnetic waves actually produced?

3. What advance was made in the use of electromagnetic waves in 1901?

4. Why was radio often called the "wireless" in its early days?

5. How does the telegraph send messages? The telephone?

6. How does radio transmit sound over long distances?

7. What term is used to describe the height of a wave? What does the term "frequency" describe?

8. What are the two types of modulation that permit electromagnetic waves to act as carriers of sound waves?

9. What are some of the special devices that had to be developed to make radio a practical reality?

10. What electronic invention was used to make these devices? How did this invention work in the radio?

11. How is an electric light bulb similar to a vacuum tube? How is it different?

12. What were two of the observations that led to the discovery of the electron by Thomson?

13. What did Fleming invent in 1904? What did this tube contain?

14. How did the diode act as a rectifier?

15. When was the triode invented? By whom?

16. What new part did the triode contain? What could it do?

17. What were some of the improvements made in vacuum tubes in the next few years?

18. How does a phototube release electrons? Why must it be used with amplifiers?

19. What is one familiar use of the phototube?

20. What is the key element in a television system?

21. How does an image orthicon tube work?

22. How is the image projected onto the screen of a television receiver?

23. How is a television image similar to a newspaper picture?

24. How does color television differ from black-and-white television?

25. What are two navigational devices that depend on electronics? What are they used for?

26. What is the echo property of waves?

27. How fast do radio waves travel? What special problem did this create in the development of radar?

28. What problem could be caused by the warm-up time needed by vacuum tubes?

29. Why was size a problem with vacuum tubes? Give an example.

30. Why were electronic devices with a large number of vacuum tubes not very reliable?

31. Why was heat a problem with vacuum tubes?

Review

A. Fill in the spaces in the following sentences with the appropriate word or phrase.

1. The _____ of a wave is a measure of the number of cycles produced per second.

2. _____ is the distance between the crest and the zero value of a wave.

3. Electromagnetic waves can act as carriers for _____ waves.

4. A device that makes the vibrations that produce electromagnetic waves is called an _____.

5. A device that increases the strength of electrical signals is called an _____.

6. A device that changes alternating current to direct current is called a _____.

7. When air and other matter have been removed from a space, a
   _____ has been created.

8. A diode contains two electrodes, the _____ and
   the _____.

9. A triode contains a third electrode which is called the
   _____.

10. Vacuum tubes work in an electric current somewhat in the
    same way as _____ that control the flow of
    liquids and gases.

11. In a _____, electrons are released by the energy
    of light.

12. _____ is a navigational system that can locate
    aircraft.

13. _____ is a navigational system that can locate
    underwater objects.

14. The basis for television is a light-sensitive vacuum tube called
    the _____.

15. The two systems for modifying radio waves to carry sound
    waves are _____ and _____.

16. Light is given off by an incandescent bulb because of
    _____ in the circuit.

B. Explain briefly some of the advantages that vacuum tubes brought
   to electrical systems. What were some of the systems and devices
   made possible by the use of vacuum tubes? What were the disadvantages of using vacuum tubes?

UNIT SEVEN
MINIATURIZATION AND
MICROMINIATURIZATION

Special Terms

Transistors: Small pieces of semiconductor material like silicon or germanium that have been treated with impurities so that they can perform the same functions as vacuum tubes.

Semiconductor: A substance with a higher resistance than a good conductor like copper, and a lower resistance than an insulator like rubber.

N Type: A semiconductor that has been treated with impurities so that it has an excess of electrons.

P Type: A semiconductor that has been treated with impurities so that there are spaces from which electrons have been removed.

Emitter/Collector/Base: The three parts of a transistor. Transistors consist of p and n type semiconductors which are arranged in either an npn or pnp structure. The middle section is called the base, and the two outer sections are the collector and the emitter.

Solid-State Electronics: The use of solid semiconductors like silicon in electronic equipment. *Solid-state physics* is the science that studies the behavior of electrons in these and other solids.

Printed Circuits: Circuits of a conducting material that are printed on sheets of insulating material in order to connect transistors attached to the sheets.

Miniaturization: The use of extremely small components such as transistors and printed circuits in electronic equipment.

77

Microminiaturization: The use of components even smaller than transistors for electronic equipment. Some of these components are only a fraction of an inch thick.

Integrated Circuits: Circuits made by placing the impurities that create *n* and *p* type semiconductors on very thin slices of silicon or other semiconducting material.

Computer: An automatic electronic device that can process information and perform calculations at a very rapid speed.

Programming: Preparing sequenced instructions that tell the computer how to process information.

Digital Computer: A computer that processes information represented in the form of *digits*—single numerals. Within the digital computer, all operations are performed in the *binary code*, in which all numbers are represented using only the digits 0 and 1.

Analog Computer: A computer used in scientific and technical work such as aircraft design, where the parts of the problem are precise measurements. It is also used for training devices involving simulation, the imitation of real conditions.

Laser Beam: A concentrated beam of light that does not spread out in the shape of a cone like ordinary beams of light.

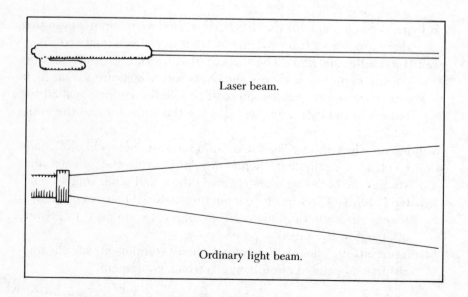

Laser beam.

Ordinary light beam.

Vocabulary Practice

1. What are *transistors*?

2. What is a *semiconductor*?

3. What is the difference between an *n type* and a *p type* semiconductor?

4. What are the three parts of a transistor called?

5. What are the two arrangements of *n* and *p* type substances in a transistor?

6. What is the subject matter of *solid-state physics*?

7. What are *printed circuits*?

8. What does the term *miniaturization* mean in the field of electronics?

9. Why is the term *microminiaturization* used now?

10. What are *integrated circuits*?

11. What is *programming*?

12. What kind of information does a *digital computer* process? What code is used within the digital computer?

13. What is an *analog computer* used for?

14. What is the difference between a *laser beam* and an ordinary beam of light?

Miniaturization and Microminiaturization

In the early days of radio, before the vacuum tube came into general use, crystals of carborundum, a compound of silicon and

A printed circuit board. (Courtesy of Western Electric Company)

carbon, were used as rectifiers. During and after World War II, electronic equipment became so important and so complex that a substitute for the vacuum tube was required for the continued growth of the field. In a sense, the answer to the problem was found in improvements in the use of crystals—vacuum tubes were replaced by *transistors* consisting basically of silicon.

Silicon is one of the substances classed as a *semiconductor*. These substances have a conductivity somewhere between good conductors like silver, copper, and aluminum, and insulators like rubber, porcelain, and glass, which permit almost no movement of electrons at all. Modern transistors are small pieces of a semiconductor material such as silicon that have been treated with impurities so that they possess free electrons at room temperature. Another material used is a metal called germanium. Germanium, however, is very rare, whereas silicon is extremely common—it is the basic element in sand. Another element, selenium, is used in light-sensitive transistors. A number of chemical compounds have also been found suitable for use in different types of transistors.

The transistor was created in 1948 by three American scientists, John Bardeen, Walter Brattain, and William Shockley. They were doing research for the Bell Telephone Laboratories, part of the corporation that owns and operates most of the telephones in the

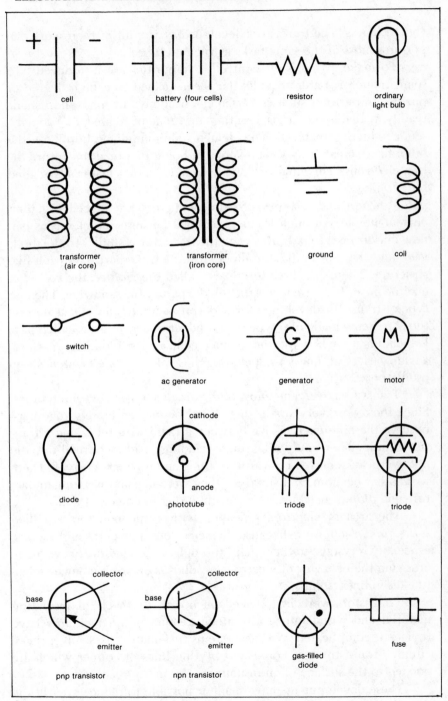

Symbols used in electrical and electronic diagrams.

United States. The transistors developed as a result of their work can perform most of the same tasks as vacuum tubes.

To make a transistor, controlled impurities are introduced into semiconductor material which has been refined to a high degree of purity. Impurities such as arsenic, antimony, or phosphorus add readily available electrons, creating an *n type* of treated, or "doped," semiconducting material. The elements aluminum and boron, on the other hand, create tiny vacant spots, or holes, that tend to capture the free electrons. This kind of doped semiconducting material is called the *p type.*

When *n* and *p* types of semiconductors are placed together, current flowing through them is rectified because the electrons can flow only from *n* to *p*. In this way, the transistor is similar to the diode vacuum tube; but unlike the diode, it has a three-part, sandwich-like structure. There are three terminals, called the *emitter*, the *collector*, and the *base*. The base forms the middle part of the sandwich. The first type of transistor developed for widespread use has an *npn* structure, the base being made of *p* type semiconductor. The other is called *pnp*. Depending upon how they are connected in a circuit, they can perform a wide variety of functions, including those of amplifiers, switches, and oscillators.

Transistors overcame most of the disadvantages of vacuum tubes. Since they were very small, they could be packed closely together—observe the difference in size between a radio with tubes and a transistor radio. They could take rough handling, seldom burned out, did not overheat, required no warm-up time, and used less current. There were other economic advantages—they were inexpensive to manufacture and did not need nearly as much wiring to connect them.

The area of electronics dealing with semiconductors is called *solid-state electronics*, because the electrons move through solids, especially crystals, rather than through a conductor or vacuum. Studying the behavior of electrons in solids is one of the newer scientific disciplines, *solid-state physics.*

Transistors were first placed on boards or sheets of insulating material and wired into a circuit. Since then *printed circuits* have replaced complicated wiring systems in many cases. In printed circuits, transistors are connected by thin lines of copper which are bonded to the surface of an insulator.

These developments have made it possible to reduce greatly the size of electronic equipment. This is known as *miniaturization.* Next, electronics moved on to *microminiaturization*, meaning equipment became still smaller (*micro* comes from the Greek word for small). Equipment for space navigation and communication systems, or for computers, required smaller, lighter, and more reliable semiconductor devices than the transistor. Scientists and engineers working together created the *integrated circuit*, in which both circuits and transistors are placed on tiny slices of silicon only a fraction of an inch thick. A piece of silicon or other semiconducting substance, called a wafer, can be cut into thousands of thin slices, or chips. Impurities are then added to them to create the desired electronic behavior. Many of the completed circuits are only a tenth of an inch square.

Microelectronics has made significant contributions toward the development of today's *computers*, machines that can process information at a high rate of speed. As we noted in the previous unit, it is possible to build a computer with vacuum tubes, but it requires a large area to contain it, special cooling devices, and frequent repairs due to burned out or defective tubes.

A bank of computers and other components in a modern computer installation.

With microminiaturization these difficulties have been over-come, making it possible to build the complex computers used in business, government, and science. They store information so that it is available for immediate use, and they do complex calculations in a fraction of a second. Pieces of information are stored in special micro-circuits. There are millions of these in the large new machines. These are the machine's memory, like the bits of information that are always available in the human brain. Other circuits perform the calculations. For all its speed and versatility, however, a computer cannot think for itself; it must be given the correct information and the correct instruc-tions in an appropriate sequence. This is called *programming*, and is a human function.

There are two types of computers. The *digital computer* is the most common. A *digit* is a number written with one symbol. The decimal system has ten digits, 0 to 9. Within the computer, informa-tion and instructions are changed into the *binary code*, a system in which all numbers are represented using only two digits, 0 and 1. These two digits correspond to millions of switches in the computer circuits that can be either on or off. The other type of computer is called the *analog computer*. It is used principally for scientific and technical problems involving actual measurements. It can also be part of a training device that makes use of simulation—imitating conditions that would occur in reality.

The developments in electronics have been so rapid that it is not possible to mention all of them here. Anything written about electron-ics will probably be at least partially out-of-date by the time it appears in print. We should mention one other new invention, however, because it has attracted so much attention. The *laser beam* (*laser* means *l*ight *a*mplification by *s*timulated *e*mission of *r*adiation) is a concentrated beam of light. It is more intense than an ordinary beam of light because it does not spread out into the shape of a cone. When the laser beam was first produced, it was simply a laboratory curiosity which had been developed without any particular practical applica-tion in mind. Since then, however, many uses have been found for it in medicine, industry, and science.

The teamwork of scientists and engineers is an important aspect of modern research. Electronics is one of the fields where this team-work is constantly achieving new and astonishing results.

Discussion

1. What did rectifiers consist of in the early days of radio?

2. What was required for the continued growth of electronics after World War II?

3. How is silicon classed in regard to electric conductivity? How are silver, copper, and aluminum classed? How are rubber, porcelain, and glass classed?

4. What are some of the substances used to make transistors?

5. When and where were transistors first created?

6. What can transistors do?

7. What happens when arsenic, antimony, or phosphorus is added to semiconducting material?

8. What is the effect of adding aluminum and boron to semiconducting material?

9. What becomes possible when *n* and *p* types of semiconductors are placed together? What other device produces the same effect?

10. What are the three terminals of a transistor? How are they put together?

11. How are the semiconductors arranged in a transistor?

12. What are the advantages of transistors over vacuum tubes?

13. What area of electronics deals with the behavior of free electrons in solids? What new scientific discipline deals with this?

14. What are printed circuits? What did they replace?

15. What has the development of transistors and printed circuits come to be called?

16. What was the next development in electronics after miniaturization?

17. What kinds of electronic equipment require still smaller semiconductor devices?

18. What did scientists and engineers create to meet this demand?

19. How are integrated circuits made? How large are they when completed?

20. What difficulties have been overcome by the use of microelectronic devices in computers?

21. What is the function of microcircuits in a computer?

22. Why is it necessary to prepare programs for a computer?

23. What kind of code is used by a digital computer? What do the numbers correspond to in the computer?

24. What is the other kind of computer? What are its principal uses?

25. What is a laser beam? For what purpose was it first invented? What uses have been found for it?

26. What is constantly achieving new and astonishing results in the field of electronics?

Review

A. Fill in the spaces in the following sentences with the appropriate word or phrase.

   1. In the _____ of treated semiconducting material, there is an excess of electrons.

2. In the _____ of treated semiconducting material, there are holes from which electrons have been removed.

3. A transistor has three terminals: the one connected to the middle part of the "sandwich" is the _____, and the two outer parts are the _____ and the _____.

4. _____ is the study of the behavior of free electrons in solids.

5. _____ and _____ are two of the elements from which transistors are made.

6. One arrangement of semiconductors in transistors is _____, and the other is _____.

7. _____ is one of the impurities that can create n type semiconducting material.

8. _____ is one of the impurities that can create p type semiconducting material.

9. The _____ computer uses a code of numbers consisting only of two characters.

10. A code based on two digits is a _____ code.

11. The _____ computer is used for simulating, or imitating, real conditions.

12. Preparing information and instructions for a computer is called _____.

13. An ordinary beam of light has the shape of a _____, but a _____ beam is concentrated and does not spread out.

B. On p.81 a number of symbols are given which are used in circuit diagrams. The same symbols are given below but in a different order. Without referring back to p.81, indicate what each one of them stands for.

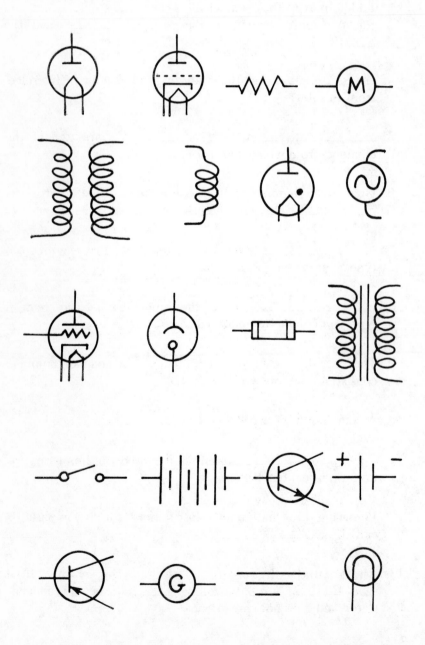

UNIT EIGHT
ELECTRICAL AND ELECTRONIC
ENGINEERING IN THE FUTURE

Special Terms

Elementary Particles: The basic components of all matter and energy not known to be combined with any other thing and believed to be incapable of subdivision.

Pulsars: Astronomical objects that emit radio waves in pulses whose rates are extremely uniform. The word comes from puls(ating) and (st)ar.

Quasars: Very distant, celestial objects that are strong radio sources with vast, unexplained energy outputs. The word comes from quas(i) and (stell)ar, meaning "like a star."

Inertial Guidance: The determination of the position or course of a ship or missile by self-contained automatic devices which detect change in direction or speed and make necessary adjustments; also called *inertial navigation.*

Hypersonic: Refers to speeds five times or greater than the speed of sound.

Cybernetics: The science of automatic controls.

Robot: An apparatus in the form of a human being that performs the mechanical functions of humans in a way that seems to show intelligence.

Information Theory: Mathematical analysis of the efficiency with which computers, telecommunication channels, and other information-processing systems are employed.

Research and Development: Investigation and experimentation by scientists, engineers, and technicians aiming for better understanding of physical laws and the development of practical systems based on such findings; often called *R&D*.

Antennae: Exposed arrangements of wires and rods which radiate and/or receive electromagnetic waves.

Filter: A device which discriminates between waves and currents, permitting the passage of some and limiting the flow of others.

Transducer: Any device which converts one form of energy to another form of energy.

Relay: An electrically operated device that opens and closes electric switches or other devices in an electric circuit.

Vocabulary Practice

1. What are *elementary particles*?

2. What are *pulsars*?

3. What are *quasars*?

4. What does an *inertial guidance* system do? What is another term often used for it?

5. What is *hypersonic* speed?

6. What is *cybernetics*?

7. What is a *robot*?

8. What is meant by *information theory*?

9. What is included in the area of *research and development*? What abbreviation is often used to refer to this area?

10. What are *antennae*? What are they used for?

11. What is a *filter*?

12. What is a *transducer?*

13. What is a *relay?*

Electrical and Electronic Engineering in the Future

So much of the development of science and technology depends on the variables of economic, political, and social developments that precise predictions about future trends in the field of electrical and electronic engineering cannot be made. But it is possible to discern certain technological trends which can reasonably be expected to occur.

Experts on the future are divided into pessimists and optimists. Pessimists forecast doom. They point to increasing pollution of the atmosphere, water, and land, the depletion of raw materials, the exhaustion of some now-common energy sources, and the geometric expansion of population.

Optimists foresee unlimited energy through harnessing the power of the atom, the discovery of new and unlimited food sources, and the dawn of an age in which human drudgery is replaced by technological advances. The truth is probably somewhere in between.

A major scientific advance such as the development of a comprehensive theory and knowledge of *elementary particles*, the basic components of all matter and energy, could profoundly change the way we live tomorrow. A theory based on knowledge of such strange objects as *pulsars*, stars that emit radio waves in uniform pulses, and *quasars*, strong radio sources and unexplained sources of enormous energy, could alter life in ways we cannot yet forecast.

Electrical and electronic scientists and engineers are engaged in examining and developing these areas. They are not restricted in their exploration to our present knowledge of space or time. With an instrument known as an electron accelerator, they probe the mysteries of the atomic nucleus, and with the radio telescope they study signals from remote regions of outer space. With computers they can store information indefinitely and with electronic circuits they can get information in a thousand-billionth of a second.

A major success such as the harnessing of thermonuclear energy produced through nuclear fusion would radically affect the development of all branches of engineering. The world would move from a state of energy scarcity to an era of inexhaustible energy resources. Given the proper economic and political circumstances, this would cause tremendous growth in science and technology.

However, if this major breakthrough does not occur, the enormous need for new energy resources will continue to grow. With the ever-increasing use of fossil fuels, the effort of much of the technological community is already directed toward the discovery of new sources of non-fossil fuels. Solar, geothermal (relating to the heat of the earth's interior), tidal, and wind sources of energy are gradually becoming more economically possible. A technological breakthrough in any one of these fields would provide research work for tens of thousands of electrical engineers. New and improved types of cells, batteries, generators, convertors, power plants, and transmission lines would have to be designed, tested, evaluated, and built in order to properly use the new source of energy.

In any case, the future of electrical and electronic engineering does not depend solely on the development of new scientific theories or the discovery of new energy sources. These engineers will be engaged in diverse technological pursuits such as the following:

Electrical and electronic engineers will be intimately involved in the development of the completely automated industrial factory. It will become possible, with the aid of electronic computers, to produce goods by teams of machines that transfer materials from one to another. In such a factory a product could be manufactured, tested, labeled, packaged, and shipped without being touched by human hands or directed by human intellect.

In the field of transportation, electrical engineers are currently engaged in developing the electric automobile, train, bus, and ship. They are designing new *inertial guidance* systems which would guide rockets and interplanetary spaceships by using devices which detect changes in speed and direction and make necessary adjustments automatically.

Fueling aircraft and spacecraft by laser beam is another possibility that will transform future travel. As light energy can be converted into other forms of energy, so could the laser beam be converted to aircraft fuel. Such a breakthrough would greatly reduce the weight of aircraft and thereby increase the probability of *hyper-*

sonic travel—travel at speeds five or more times greater than the speed of sound. Planes could travel at 4,000 to 5,000 miles an hour and at altitudes of 150,000 feet.

Society will become more and more computerized, and the electronic engineer will be called upon to design and build ever-smaller computers capable of doing more varied and more complicated tasks. At some time in the future, fully automatic automobiles and homes will be built and directed by computers. Computers that "think," that learn from errors and never make the same mistake twice, that are able to repair themselves and reproduce themselves, may be the reality of tomorrow.

Cybernetics, the science of automatic controls, could eventually produce a race of *robots*—machines in human shapes that perform human tasks with what parallels human intelligence. Only human sensitivity, emotion, and sexuality will be missing. The necessary scientific knowledge for building these labor-replacing devices is available to engineers today: computer technology, microcircuit technology, control theory, and *information theory*—a mathematical analysis of the efficiency with which computers, telecommunication channels, and other information-processing systems are employed. The electronic engineer need only translate today's knowledge into tomorrow's machinery.

The exciting field of biomedical engineering offers enormous possibilities. More and more electronic instruments to extend, repair, and improve upon physical life are currently being developed. Lasers are already used to join living tissues such as detached eye retinas; their uses in surgery too intricate and delicate for the knife will become commonplace. Computers will be developed to diagnose and treat disease. Electronic engineers will devise more usable and varied organs and organ replacements. There is, theoretically, no limit to the uses of electronics in medicine.

Not only will the new developments make use of the electronic engineer; he or she will develop new electronic products for people to buy. Telephones with picture screens on which the connected parties can see each other and three-dimensional television which would completely envelop the viewer could become ordinary household items.

Research and development, or *R & D*—investigation and experimentation by scientists, engineers, and technicians—is not confined to sciences such as physics or radio astronomy. Countless engineers will continue to design and improve upon existing vacuum tubes, switches, and electromechanical devices. Improvements will be made in *antennae*, arrangements of wires and rods which fan out to receive electromagnetic waves; *filters*, which block out selected waves or current; *transducers*, which convert one form of energy to another; and *relays*, which electrically cause switches in a circuit to open and close. These are the basic components of the electronics industry and a vital segment of the industries that maintain our economy.

These exciting possibilities indicate a bright future for electrical and electronic engineers. They will play a central role in formulating, shaping, and bringing into being the immediate and distant future.

Discussion

1. What factors make it especially difficult to predict the future development of science and technology?

2. Describe a pessimistic view of the future. Describe an optimistic view of the future.

3. What do we know about pulsars? quasars?

4. What instrument is available for probing the atomic nucleus?

5. What instrument is used for receiving signals from outer space?

6. How long can a computer store information?

7. How fast can an electronic circuit act?

8. What changes might occur if thermonuclear energy were harnessed for use?

9. What are some potential sources of energy which could replace fossil fuels?

10. What would have to be improved in order to properly use a new source of energy?

11. How would a completely automated industrial factory work?

12. Why would inertial guidance be an advantage for interplanetary travel?

13. How would fueling aircraft with laser beams change travel?

14. In what sense may computers "think" in the future?

15. What science could produce a race of robots?

16. What scientific knowledge is available today which would contribute to building robots?

17. How is electronics used in the field of medicine today? What contributions will electronics make in the future?

18. What new electronic products will we be able to buy?

19. What basic components of the electronics industry will be improved in the future?

Review

Complete the following sentences by writing in a word or phrase.

1. Experts on the future are divided into _____ and _____.

2. _____ are stars that emit uniform radio waves.

3. Computers can store _____ indefinitely.

4. Some of the new sources of energy that may become feasible are _____, _____, _____, and _____.

5. In a fully automated factory, products could be manufactured, _____, _____, packaged, and _____ without being touched by human hands.

6. Fueling aircraft and spacecraft by _____ would greatly reduce their weight.

7. Computers will become _____ and able to do _____ tasks.

8. Robots will be able to perform _____ tasks with what seems like human _____.

9. In the field of medicine, _____ will be used for surgery too delicate for the knife.

10. Telephones may have _____.

11. Television will become _____.

12. R&D will continue to deal with existing electronic components such as _____, _____, _____, and _____.

13. The future of electrical and electronic engineering seems _____ _____.

INDEX
OF SPECIAL TERMS

AC	27	DIGITAL COMPUTER	78
ALTERNATING CURRENT	27	DIODE	65
AMP	26	DIRECT CURRENT	27
AMPERAGE	26	ELECTODES	15
AMPERE	26	ELECTROLYSIS	15
AMPLIFIER	65	ELECTROLYTE	15
AMPLITUDE	65	ELECTROLYTIC PROCESS	15
AMPLITUDE MODULATION	65	ELECTROMAGNETIC WAVES	64
ANALOG COMPUTER	78	ELECTROMAGNETISM	40
ANODE	15	ELECTROMOTIVE FORCE	26
ANTENNAE	90	ELECTRON	2,14
AQUEDUCT	3	ELECTRON FLOW	26
ARMATURE	40	ELECTRON MICROSCOPE	2
ATOM	2	ELEMENTARY PARTICLES	89
ATOMIC FISSION	54	EMF	26
ATOMIC FUSION	54	EMITTER/COLLECTOR/BASE	77
ATOMIC NUMBER	14	EMPIRICAL INFORMATION	3
BINARY CODE	78	ENERGY	15
CATHODE	15	ENGINEER	1
CELL/BATTERY	15	ENGINEERING	1
CHARGE	14	FILTER	90
CHEMICAL ENGINEERING	2	FREE ELECTRONS	14
CIRCUIT	15	FREQUENCY	65
CIVIL ENGINEERING	1	FREQUENCY MODULATION	65
COIL	40	FRICTION	14
COMMUTATOR	41	FUSE	27
COMPUTER	78	GENERATOR	41
CONDUCTOR	14	GRID	65
CORPUSCLE	54	GROUND	27
CREST	65	GROUNDING	27
CURRENT	15	HIGH VACUUM	65
CURRENT FLOW	26	HYPERSONIC	89
CYBERNETICS	89	IMAGE ORTHICON TUBE	66
DC	27	INCANDESCENT LIGHT	54
DIGIT	78	INERTIAL GUIDANCE	89

INERTIAL NAVIGATION	89	POSITIVE	14
INFORMATION THEORY	89	PRIMARY COIL/SECONDARY COIL	41
INSULATOR	14	PRINTED CIRCUITS	77
INTEGRATED CIRCUITS	78	PROFESSION	1
KILOVOLT	54	PROGRAMMING	78
KILOWATT	27	PROTON	14
KILOWATT HOUR	27	PULSARS	89
KINETIC ENERGY	54	QUANTIFICATION	3
KW	27	QUASARS	89
KWH	27	RADAR	66
LASER BEAM	78	RADIO WAVES	54, 64
LINES OF FORCE	40	RECHARGING	15
MAGNET	40	RECTIFIER	54
MAGNETIC FIELD	40	RELAY	90
MAGNETISM	40	RESEARCH AND DEVELOPMENT	90
MECHANICAL ENGINEERING	2	RESISTANCE	26
MEGAWATT	27	ROBOT	89
MICROMINIATURIZATION	78	ROTOR	41
MILITARY ENGINEERING	1	SEMICONDUCTOR	54, 77
MINIATURIZATION	77	SERIES CIRCUIT	27
MINING AND METALLURGY	1	SERIES PARALLEL CIRCUIT	27
MODULATION	65	SHORT CIRCUIT	27
N TYPE	77	SOLID-STATE ELECTRONICS	77
NEGATIVE	14	SOLID-STATE PHYSICS	77
NEUTRON	14	SONAR	66
NORTH POLE/SOUTH POLE	40	STATIC ELECTRICITY	14
NPN	77	STATOR	41
NUCLEAR ENGINEERING	2	STEP-DOWN TRANSFORMER	41
NUCLEAR FISSION	54	STEP-UP TRANSFORMER	41
NUCLEAR FUSION	54	SUBATOMIC PARTICLES	2
NUCLEI	2	TERMINAL	15
NUCLEUS	2	THERMOCOUPLE	55
OHM	26	THERMOELECTRICITY	55
OHM'S LAW	26	TRANSDUCER	90
OSCILLATE	65	TRANSFORMER	41
OSCILLATOR	65	TRANSISTORS	77
P TYPE	77	TRIODE	65
PARALLEL CIRCUIT	27	TURBINE	41
PARTICLE ACCELERATOR	3	V	26
PETROLEUM ENGINEERING	2	VACUUM	54
PHOTOELECTRICITY	55	VACUUM TUBE	65
PHOTOTUBE	65	VOLT	26
PIEZOELECTRICITY	55	VOLTAGE	26
PLANETARY ELECTRONS	14	WATT	27
PNP	77	ZERO VALUE	65